FOUR OTHER GOSPELS

Shadows on the Contours of Canon

by

JOHN DOMINIC CROSSAN

A Seabury Book
WINSTON PRESS
Minneapolis • Chicago • New York

Library of Congress Catalog Card Number: 84–52137

ISBN: 0–86683–959–3

Printed in the United States of America

5 4 3 2 1

Winston Press, 430 Oak Grove,
Minneapolis, MN 55403

CONTENTS

PROLOGUE

METHOD AND EMPHASIS

The method I use in this book is a fairly standard scholarly one. It is variously termed tradition-critical or traditio-historical or history-of-traditions analysis. I prefer to avoid hyphens and call it simply transmissional analysis. But it has not been underlined as much as it should have been in past scholarship that *exactly the same transmissional analysis can be the basis for three quite different transmissional emphases.* This prologue will explore those three options in both their adequacy and their implications. What is significant, however, in a scholar's work is not the use of transmissional analysis but which transmissional *emphasis* is derived from that analysis.

Primal Emphasis

In primal emphasis the concern is with the original words or deeds of Jesus, with what actually happened for its own sake. It is vastly imprudent to speak of *ipsissima verba*, that is, the precise and verbatim words of Jesus, since Jesus was an oral teacher and within such a sensibility one can speak only of original structure rather than original syntax. Indeed, true oral sensibility could be defined as the triumph of structure over syntax, of linguistic structure over sequential syntax.

A scholar interested in primal emphasis seeks to recover that original word or deed, teaching or event. The function of the transmissional analysis is to remove what later writers have added in order to see again that original moment. Such an emphasis may speak quite pejoratively of those additions, may call them changes or alterations, cobwebs or debris. But, in any case, they are studied only to be removed.

A primal emphasis cannot be dismissed simply because it concerns a scholarly reconstruction. If reconstruction alone

7

invalidated it, much more would be thereby invalidated as well, for example, the very Greek text of the New Testament itself.

Final Emphasis

In final emphasis the concern is with the ultimate text present on the page. A scholar, for example, might undertake a transmissional analysis not because of any primal emphasis but in order to understand genetically what a given author actually and finally produced. Indeed, a final emphasis may sometimes even dismiss the whole idea of transmissional analysis and claim exclusive concern with the text as it now stands in final context. This is probably not a good strategy, however, because one tends at least to look from the corner of the eye at those other versions. Can one really speak of "The Lord's Prayer" without facing the fact that there are two versions of it within the New Testament itself? Can one really speak of "The Beatitudes" without facing the fact that there are two versions of them within the New Testament itself?

Hermeneutical Emphasis

Both those previous emphases were on product, on either the primal and original product at the time of the historical Jesus, or the final and scribal product at the time of the individual evangelist. The third emphasis is not on product but on process, not on initial or terminal product but on the entire process which flows from one to the other and which may even have started before them and certainly continues after them. I term it hermeneutical emphasis and I consider that it is the only adequate emphasis in dealing with the Jesus tradition. This can be seen by comparing it with the two preceding emphases and by underlining their weaknesses in comparision with it.

Take, for example, a parable of Jesus. Imagine that we have carefully reconstructed the plot outline of Jesus' original parable by removing from it what is proper to the intracanonical or extracanonical versions. What we have removed are not accretions and alterations but interpretations and applications. It is the intrinsic nature of the successful parable not just to be repeated but to be interpreted. The genre itself provokes hermeneutics, and multiple interpretations are intrinsic to its being. The fact that interpretations are given internally and textually rather than externally and contextually is of minor importance. They are the parable's destiny and, having carefully removed them, we would have immediately to restore them. In parable, original product includes hermeneutical process. And what is true of the words of Jesus' teaching is equally true of the events of Jesus' life.

A similar problem arises with final emphasis. First of all, we have extracanonical and intracanonical interpretations. Can one simply ignore the former as having no bearing on the latter? And even if one could, what of those cases where there are divergent interpretations within the intracanonical books themselves. It is not possible to discuss multiple versions within the canon without raising the problem of hermeneutical process. Once again, a product emphasis is inadequate within a situation of hermeneutical process. Indeed, one begins to suspect that what has been canonized by such multiple interpretations of the same parable or the same event is not this or that interpreation but the very necessity of interpretation itself.

Primal emphasis is sometimes called historical, and final emphasis is sometimes called canonical. But not even those terms can save both emphases from being ultimately absorbed within a hermeneutical emphasis. The modes and genres of Jesus' language, such as, for example, the parable or the aphorism, render hermeneutics imperative, so that transmissional analysis which is both historical and canonical becomes eventually and necessarily hermeneutical analysis. And once the parables of Jesus initiated that process it was possible to apply it as well to the Jesus of the parables himself.

Hermeneutics is the Beatrice of this book and transmissional analysis is her handmaiden. My fascination is with the ways in which the hermeneutical processes initiated by the parables of Jesus were turned eventually on Jesus himself. What was provoked by his speech was unleashed on his life.

CORPUS AND CANON

The corpus I use in this book is extensively mutilated and alarmingly accidental. These other gospels were all discovered within the last one hundred years, are all save one quite fragmentary, and all owe their discovery as much to chance as to science. Yet these four extracanonical gospels are the ones I consider most important to place in dialectic with the four intracanonical ones. It is probably fair to say that most scholars ignore their existence. They have been buried respectfully in volumes such as the *New Testament Apocrypha* and thence issue forth only periodically as footnoted phantoms, pale ghosts that haunt the corridors of canon.

Christianity chose to base itself on a closed sequence of sacred books and to call them its Old Testament and its New Testament. By that choice it wagered its future destiny on those specific texts and on the interpretations that could be found within and between them. Given that biblical foundation, no Christian need explain an interest in the documents of the canon. But why bother with these other documents, with these other gospels? Why bother with what was left out, especially if it was deliberately left out?

The canon is neither a total nor a random collection of early Christian texts. It is both deliberate and selective and it excludes just as surely as it includes. I would even say that you cannot understand what is included in the canon unless you understand what was excluded from it. When the four other gospels are played over against the four canonical gospels, both the products and the processes of those latter texts appear in a radically different light.

This book will demand close, careful, and comparative readings from the gospels with which it is concerned. But it is not intended for specialists and for scholars. It is written for anyone who takes seriously the gospel foundations of Christianity. It is written for anyone who wants to understand how, why, and whence those texts were composed. It is written for anyone who wants to know the nature of the gospel texts and who believes that inaugural moments are normative for present and future destiny.

The core challenge of the book is this. Anyone, and not just the specialist, who is willing to do careful textual comparison between the four canonical gospels and these four other gospels will never see the former the same way again. There will also be a few other things that will never look quite the same again. Among them will be, history, hermeneutics, and gospel truth.

Part One

THE GOSPEL OF THOMAS

"I took My place in the midst of the world, and I appeared to them in flesh. I found all of them intoxicated; I found none of them thirsty. And My soul became afflicted for the sons of men, because they are blind in their hearts and do not have sight; for empty they came into the world, and empty too they seek to leave the world. But for the moment they are intoxicated. When they shake off their wine, then they will repent."

Gos. Thom. 28

1 THE GOSPEL OF THOMAS
INTRODUCTION

James M. Robinson said of the collection of ancient manuscripts discovered near Nag Hammadi in December of 1945 that, "the American public at large, to the extent it has heard about this discovery at all, probably knows of it only in terms of *The Gospel of Thomas*, one of the few texts published relatively early (1959). This collection of some 114 sayings attributed to Jesus is certainly the most important part of the library for understanding the historical Jesus and the beginnings of Christianity. It alone would make the Nag Hammadi library a very important discovery, probably doing more as a single text to advance our understanding of the historical Jesus and of the transmissions of his teachings than all the Dead Sea Scrolls put together" (1979:201–2). Be that as it may, and however one judges the importance of this gospel's content, the story of its discovery must begin earlier than 1945 and elsewhere than Nag Hammadi.

DISCOVERY
The Gospel of Thomas in the Oxyrhynchus Papyri

In 1897 London's Egypt Exploration Fund which had been sponsoring archeological research since 1883 created a special subsection called the Graeco-Roman Research Account dedicated to the discovery and dissemination of remains from both classical antiquity and early Christianity in Egypt. One of the new fund's primary aims was to publish the vast hoard of manuscript fragments discovered by two Oxford scholars,

15

Bernard P. Grenfell and Arthur S. Hunt, while excavating for the society that same year at El Bahnasa.

This is the site in their own words. "On the edge of the Libyan desert, 120 miles south of Cairo, a series of low mounds, covered with Roman and early Arab pottery, marks the spot where stood the capital of the Oxyrhynchite nome. The wide area of the site, and the scale of the buildings and city walls, where traceable, testify to its past size and importance; but it declined rapidly after the Arab conquest, and its modern representative, Behnesa, is a mere hamlet. [It was] a flourishing city in Roman times, and one of the chief centres of early Christianity in Egypt" (Grenfell & Hunt, 1897:5).

An initial three weeks' work in the ancient cemetery produced very little but when they turned to the town's rubbish-dumps they found papyri fragments, extensive in quantity, in variety of subject, and in time, ranging from the first to the eighth centuries of our era. Among these manuscripts, and discovered at the very start of the excavation so that it was given pride of place as Oxyrhynchus Papyrus 1, was the papyrus fragment with which we are concerned.

Oxy P 1. The fragment, now in Oxford's Bodleian Library, was slightly smaller than a four by six inch index card, was written in medium uncials with a single column on both sides, was broken off across the bottom of the column, was numbered in the top right-hand corner as page eleven, and was thus clearly part of a codex rather than a scroll.

What of its date? The external evidence from other fragments found alongside it and the internal evidence from the handwriting, the codex format, and the presence of standard abbreviations found in biblical manuscripts indicate that "the date therefore probably falls within the period 150–300 A.D." and, if one wishes to be more specific, "the papyrus was probably written not much later than the year 200" (Grenfell & Hunt: 1897:6). This gives, of course, only the date when the papyrus document was written down and not the date when the content itself was first composed. On this latter point, the fragment's discoverers had four conclusions: "(1) that we have here part of a collection of sayings, not extracts from a narrative gospel; (2) that they were not heretical; (3) that they were independent of the Four Gospels in their present shape; (4) that they were earlier than 140 A.D., and might go back to the first century" (Grenfell & Hunt: 1898:2).

We know, as they could not have known, that the eight sayings on their fragment represented what we today number as *Gos. Thom.* 26 (end), 27, 28 (start) on the front and 29(end), 30+77b, 31, 32, 33 (start) on the back. Nevertheless, those four conclusions above can still stand as a description of what we now know as the *Gospel of Thomas.*

Oxy P 654. "By a curious stroke of good fortune our second excavations at Oxyrhynchus were, like the first, signalized by the discovery of a fragment of a collection of Sayings of Jesus. This consists of forty-two incomplete lines on the verso of a survey-list of various pieces of land, thus affording another example of the not uncommon practice of using the back of ephemeral documents for literary texts" (Grenfell & Hunt: 1904a:1).

This second fragment, now in London's British Museum, was about three by ten inches, was complete at the top but broken off both at the bottom and along the right borders of the column, was written in medium uncials at the middle or end of the third century, and was part of a papyrus roll rather than a codex.

The original finders recognized the high probability that their second season had turned up the start of that very collection from which their first season had already found an extract. They also maintained that the four conclusions proposed earlier for Oxy P 1 still held firm after the discovery of Oxy P 654. We now know, of course, that they had found the Prologue and first seven sayings of the *Gospel of Thomas.*

Oxy P 655. Grenfell and Hunt had called Oxy P 1 and 654,

"Sayings of Jesus." In their second season they had also found what they termed a "Fragment of a Lost Gospel" (1904a:22; 1904b:37). This document, now in Harvard's Houghton Library, was actually eight fragments, denominated a, b, c, d, e, f, g, h, from a papyrus scroll written in small uncials. The largest one was slightly over three inches square and contained the middle of two narrow columns. The smaller fragments were not actually connected to this larger unit but Grenfell and Hunt attempted to reconstruct them as if they all came from the tops or bottoms of those two columns.

For the date of the manuscript, the original finders concluded that although they "would not assign it to the second century, it is not likely to have been written later than A.D. 250" (Grenfell & Hunt, 1904a:23). Since the five sayings in Oxy P 655 happened to lack any of the "Jesus says" openings characteristic of Oxy P 1 and 654, Grenfell and Hunt failed to realize that it was part of the same collection of sayings as in those other fragments. We now know that they had discovered *Gos. Thom.* 24 in fragment d and *Gos. Thom.* 36–39 in fragments a, b, c. Fragments e, f, g, h are probably two small for even present identification.

The Gospel of Thomas
in the Nag Hammadi Codices

The town of Nag Hammadi is located about 370 miles south of Cairo where the paved road and railroad tracks cross over between the west and east banks of the Nile. There is a large eastward bulge in the Nile between Nag Hammadi and Luxor, about eighty miles to the south, so that at Nag Hammadi the Nile is actually flowing from east to west. In the small but fertile area between that eastward flow of the Nile and the cliffs of the Jabal al-Tarif to its north lies an area of great importance for the history of early Christianity in Egypt. To the west at ancient Chenoboskia, modern al-Qasr, St. Pachomius, the founder of Egyptian monasticism, was converted to Christianity and later established a monastery. And to the east at ancient Pabau, modern Faw Qibli, was the monastery and basilica which formed the headquarters of the Pachomian monastic movement. Both those sites are closer to the river than to the cliffs but it was at the base of the Jabal al-Tarif that a full Coptic text of the *Gospel of Thomas* was discovered buried among the Nag Hammadi Codices in 1945.

It is hard to overestimate the role played by James M. Robinson, Director of the Institute for Christianity and Antiquity of the Claremont Graduate School, California, in bringing the Nag Hammadi Codices into the public domain. We are equally in his debt for reconstructing the history of the library's discovery and what follows is derived totally from his own account of that detective work in Egypt (Robinson, 1979b).

Finders. Each December farmers from the region of Nag Hammadi collect the nitrate-rich soil fallen and accumulated at the base of the Jabal al-Tarif and transport it in the saddlebags of their camels to fertilize their fields. Three of the sons of Ali Muhammad Khalifah of the al-Samman clan from al-Qasr went with four others to the Nile-side cliffs on such a mission in December of 1945. Buried under a broken boulder at the base of the cliffs they discovered a large jar about two feet high with its opening closed by a bowl sealed to it by bitumen. The oldest son, Muhammad, took over, broke the jar with his mattock, and disappointed them all by finding not the hoped-for treasure but a dozen fragile books wrapped in leather covers.

Since the number of codices was fewer than enough for each camel driver to receive 2, Muhammad Ali prepared seven lots each consisting of a complete codex and parts of the others torn up for this purpose. . . . The other camel drivers, ignorant of the value inferent in the codices and fearing both sorcery and Muhammad Ali, renounced their claims to a share. He then stacked the lots back together in a pile, unwound his white headdress, knotted them in it, and slung the whole bundle over his shoulder. Unhobbling his camel, he rode back to his home in al-Qasr, in the courtyard of which the animals were kept and bread baked in the large clay oven. Here he dumped the codices, loose leaves and fragments, on the ground

19

among the straw that was lying by the oven to be burned. [His mother] Umm Ahmad has conceded that she burned much of the ripped-out papyrus and broken covers of [Codices] XI and XII, in the oven along with the straw (Robinson, 1979b:214).

It seems clear that the library suffered far more loss and damage immediately after its discovery than during its long sojourn in the sand.

Dealers. At this point, with poor Muhammad Ali scarce able to give away the codices, the middlemen began to appear on the scene. Their escapades have been told by Robinson in exquisite if not excruciating detail (see 1979b:214–24) and it suffices here to note a few highlights. Codex III was sold to the Coptic Museum in Cairo by Raghib, a circuit teacher of history and English in the Coptic parochial schools. The Registry of Acquisitions dates the transaction to 4 October 1946 and this Arabic entry gave Robinson the essential lead for tracking down the participants and reconstructing the events. Most of Codex I was sold by Albert Eid, a Belgian antiquities dealer in Cairo, to the Jung Institute in Zurich. But the majority of the codices found their way into the possession of a Cypriot antiquities dealer named Phocion Tano in Cairo. Eventually these were all commandeered and nationalized by the Egyptian government, and, with the return of Codex I from abroad, the entire library was reassembled in the Coptic Museum in Old Cairo.

Scholars. Here are the statistics. The recovered library contained twelve books or codices (I-XII) and eight leaves which had been removed from another (XIII) and placed within the front cover of Codex VI before the library's burial long ago. Apart from Codex X, all of the codices contain more than one treatise or tractate. This can be as high as eight tractates in Codex VI. Altogether there are fifty-two tractates within the thirteen codices. Some of these are duplicates so that there are actually forty-six separate treatises. Of these six were extant even before Nag Hammadi. That brings us to forty texts which were lost, save for small unrecognized fragments, before the present discovery. As Robinson sums it up, "it would be safe to think of the Nag Hammadi library as adding to the amount of literature that has survived from antiquity thirty more-or-less complete texts, and ten more that are fragmentary" (*NHLE:* 12).

Here are the publications. The first and most important one is *The Facsimile Edition of the Nag Hammadi Codices,* published under the auspices of the Department of Antiquities of the Arab Republic of Egypt in conjunction with the United Nations Educational, Scientific and Cultural Organization. This beautiful edition was prepared by the International Committee for the Nag Hammadi Codices with James M. Robinson as Permanent Secretary and was published in twelve volumes between 1972 and 1984 by E. J. Brill of Leiden in Holland. It contains collotype reproductions in actual size of all folios of the thirteen codices, reproductions of the covers, photographs previously taken of fragments since lost, and a general introduction. The second most important publication is the multi-volume *The Coptic Gnostic Library,* edited with English translation, introduction, and notes, under the auspices of The Institute for Antiquity and Christianity, and appearing since 1975 in the Brill series "Nag Hammadi Studies." This publication includes not only the Nag Hammadi Codices themselves but other Coptic Gnostic works previously discovered, such as Papyrus Berolinensis 8502, the Askew Codex, and the Bruce Codex. The third most important publication is *The Nag Hammadi Library in English,* edited by Marvin W. Meyer, published by Harper & Row in 1977, and herein cited as *NHLE.* This single volume gives the translations and abbreviated introductions from *The Coptic Gnostic Library* just mentioned. With those three publications the Nag Hammadi Codices enter fully into the public domain for the English-speaking world. This is, of course, but the end of the beginning.

Monks. Letters used as scrap papyrus to stiffen the leather covers of the codices give dates in the first half of the fourth

√

century and this helps to date the manuscripts in that general period. Even more interestingly, that scrap papyrus suggests that the codices may have been prepared in the nearby Pachomian monasteries and this furnishes at least an hypothesis about their history.

Frederik Wisse, a member of the Coptic Gnostic Library Project of the Institute for Antiquity and Christianity, outlines the proposal as follows:

> In the middle of the fourth century, i.e., the approximate time when a number of the Nag Hammadi codices were constructed, monks in the Pachomian monasteries were able to produce and use books which included gnostic and other unorthodox material. At least twelve such codices were at one point collected and carefully buried in a jar away from the monasteries. The occasion was most likely one of the purges of heretical books instigated by the Alexandrian Patriarch. We know of such a purge under abbot Theodore, the successor of Pachomius, in response to Athanasius' anti-heretical Paschal letter of 367 A.D. . . . There is good reason to believe that concern about heresy was much less deeply and concretely felt by the Pachomian monks than by the church hierarchy in Alexandria. . . . For the monks the main issue was not orthodoxy but orthopraxy, i.e., practicing asceticism and humility as prescribed in the monastic rules. In that context orthodoxy and heresy were only of importance in their relationship with the Alexandrian church hierarchy (1978:436–37).

Monks whose main interest was practice rather than theory may well have buried their endangered library and let its serene eclecticism witness across the centuries to that primacy of concern.

The Gospel of Thomas in Greek and Coptic

At the turn of the century, then, fragments from three different Greek copies of the *Gospel of Thomas* were discovered in manuscripts dating from the start, middle, and end of the third century. The original excavators and editors could not have known that they had discovered in whole or in part what we now number as that gospel's Prologue and sayings 1, 2, 3, 4, 5,

6, 7, 24, 26, 27, 28, 29, 30+77b, 31, 32, 33, 36, 37, 38, 39. It may also be said that the four conclusions they drew in 1897–88 on the strength of Oxy P 1 alone are far more correct than many conclusions others drew later when the complete *Gospel of Thomas* became available in Coptic.

This complete version is a translation from Greek into Coptic, that is, Egyptian written with the Greek alphabet and seven other special letters. It now forms the second tractate of Codex II in the Nag Hammadi Library and is very well preserved although with some damage to the bottom and top outside corners of each page.

Once the Greek and Coptic texts were recognized as the same *Gospel of Thomas* close comparisons became possible and certain conclusions became evident. J. A. Fitzmyer's detailed analysis noted that, "while in most cases we found an almost word-for-word identity between the Greek and Coptic versions, there are some differences which force us to conclude that we are not dealing with the same recension of the *Gospel according to Thomas* in the two languages. ... Though it is possible that another Greek recension existed, of which the Coptic is a faithful rendering, it is much more likely that the Coptic version is an adapted translation" (416).

PROVENANCE

If we go back before scholars, dealers, finders, and monks, what about the origens of this *Gospel of Thomas?*

Judas the Twin. The most important indication of provenance is the very peculiar name of its apostolic author, Judas the Twin, which in Greek is Judas Didymos, in Aramaic is Judas Thomas, and in bilingual redundancy is Judas Thomas Didymos or some such triad. On the one hand, this conjunction of Judas Thomas-Didymos never appears in the New Testament. In John 11:16; 20:24; 21:2 the name is "Thomas, called Didymos." And in John 14:22 when he is called Judas he is identified simply as "Judas (not Iscariot)." On the other hand, one of the Old Syriac translations of John 14:22 gives that as "Judas Thomas." That points the way towards Syriac-speaking Syria as the geographical area where Thomas the Twin was of supreme importance. But this can be specified even more closely because it was around Edessa, situated on the Euphrates tributary, the Daisan, that this apostle was known precisely as Judas the Twin (brother of Jesus).

Edessa. This is a summary of Edessan history in the first Christian centuries as given by L. W. Barnard (161–62):

> Edessa was the capital of the small principality of Osrhoene east of the Euphrates and it lay on the great trade route to the East which passed between the Syrian desert to the South and the mountains of Armenia to the North. The city's inhabitants spoke Syriac, an Aramaic dialect akin to, but not identical with, that spoken in Palestine; and this dialect was the medium of commerce in the Euphrates valley. The city was a centre of literary culture long before the coming of Christianity and its earliest surviving documents have about them an ease and fluidity, perhaps reflecting traces of Greek influence, which is not lost in modern translation. The external history of Edessa was that of many another border state. When the Seleucid Empire was divided between Rome and Parthia Osrhoene lay on the frontier outside the confines of the Empire and within Parthian suzerainty. In Trajan's time c. 116 Edessa was stormed and sacked by the Roman General Lusius Quietus and this was the beginning of the end of its independence. The superior power of Rome exacted a reluctant homage and, after the conclusion of the Parthian war under Marcus Aurelius, forts were constructed and a Roman garrison stationed in the town of Nisibis [east of Edessa]. The princes of Osrhoene attempted, without avail, to shake off the yoke and eventually in 216 Abgar IX, King of Edessa, was sent in chains to Rome and his dominions reduced to a Roman province.

It is here in Edessa that an apostle was revered and remembered precisely as Judas the Twin, "twin brother of Christ, apostle of the Most High and fellow-initiate into the hidden word of Christ, who dost receive his secret sayings," as he is addressed in the *Acts of Thomas* 39 (*NTA*: 2.464). And it is here in Edessa that his remains were believed to rest from the fourth century onwards (Bauer: 11).

The Thomas Tradition. There are four main documents involved. First, there is the *Gospel of Thomas*. In the Prologue, the Coptic says, "These are the secret sayings which the living Jesus spoke and which Didymos Judas Thomas wrote down." The reconstructed Greek text of Oxy P 654 says, "These are the [secret] words [which] the living Jesus [sp]oke, an[d Judas who] (is) also (called) Thomas [wrote (them) down]." Thus the writer is identified as Judas the Twin, Judas Thomas/Didymos. Second, there is the *Book of Thomas the Contender*, the final tractate from the same Codex II of Nag Hammadi. The first part of this is a dialogue between Jesus and Judas and this probably dates from the end of the second century (Turner: 237). Thomas is the usual name for the apostle throughout the dialogue but he is identified at the start as "Judas Thomas" and near the end as "Judas—the one called Thomas" (*NHLE*: 188,192). Third, there is the third-century *Acts of Thomas* which tells how the apostles "divided the regions of the world, that each one of us might go to the region which fell to his lot, and to the nation to which the Lord sent him. According to lot, India fell to Judas Thomas, who is also (called) Didymus." A few lines later he is called simply "Thomas" and then soon after he is "Judas, who is also (called) Thomas" (*NTA*: 2.443). Those first three documents are all linked by traditions concerning the apostle precisely as Judas the Twin and the next one links this same figure to Edessa itself. Fourth, then, there is the Abgar legend through which fourth century Catholic Christianity pressed its claims against Gnostic Christianity in Edessa by maintaining that Thaddeus (Addai), and not Thomas, was the first apostle of that eastern Syrian capital city. This magnificent piece of documentary impertinence said that King Abgar wrote Jesus inviting him to Edessa and he wrote back that he would send him an apostle later on. We first hear of this interchange from Eusebius around 325 A.D. He says he saw both letters in the church archives at

Edessa and another document which claimed that, "After the Ascension of Jesus, Judas who is also called Thomas sent to him the apostle Thaddaeus, one of the seventy" (*NTA:* 1.442). The same story appears in *The Teaching of Addai* from around 400 A.D. but this has nothing about a letter of Jesus, just an oral response. Once again we read that, "After the Messiah had ascended to heaven Judas Thomas sent Addai, the apostle, one of the seventy-two apostles, to Abgar" (Howard: 11). Here again the name is Judas Thomas and it is interesting that even though catholicism wishes to link Edessan Christianity directly to Jesus through Thaddaeus, it still finds it necessary to mention Judas Thomas as the one who actually sent Thaddaeus.

In tradition and counter-tradition, then, and across possibly even the first to the fourth centuries, it is Judas the Twin, Judas Thomas/Didymos, who is the ancient apostle of Edessa. In the words of Helmut Koester, "this proves that the Thomas tradition was the oldest form of Christianity in Edessa, antedating the beginning of both Marcionite and orthodox Christianity in that area" (Robinson & Koester: 129). It also proves that the original provenance of the *Gospel of Thomas* was neither Oxyrhynchus nor Nag Hammadi in Egypt but Edessa, the blessed city, situated inside the curve of the Euphrates in eastern Syria.

CONTENT

Christianity in Edessa, separated at its inception by Syriac language and Parthian hegemony, went its own most particular way. Eastern Syriac-speaking Christianity was not western Greek-speaking Christianity, and the Daisan did not flow as easily as the Orontes into the Tiber. This must be emphasized in evaluating the content of the *Gospel of Thomas*.

Literary Structure

The gospel is composed exclusively of aphorisms, parables, and dialogues of Jesus and is thus a discourse rather than a narrative gospel. On the one hand, that distinguishes it from the four intracanonical narrative gospels, but, on the other, the fact that it is the earthly Jesus who is speaking or replying (see 22, 60, 100), clearly distinguishes it from other discourse gospels at Nag Hammadi where it is the resurrected Jesus who speaks and replies to the apostles.

The units of the gospel, which scholarship numbers as 1–114, usually begin with "Jesus said" or "He said" (1, 8, 65, 74) but sometimes they begin with questions, comments, or requests from the disciples in general (6, 12, 18, 20, 24, 37, 43, 51, 52, 53, 99, 113) or particular disciples such as Mary (21), Salome (61), or Simon Peter (114), or more vaguely from "a man" (72), "a woman" (79), or "they said" (91, 104). It is also worth noting how some sayings have at least minimal narrative features (see 22, 60, 100).

Internally, the units may be composed of just a single saying or they may have two, three, or even four indpedendent sayings combined in a single unit (see 21). Externally, there is no overall compositional design evident in the gospel. Many of the units are linked together verbally or formally but only in small clusters of two or three units. There is, for example, a verbal cluster in 73–74–75:

> Jesus said, "The harvest is great but the laboreres are few.
> Beseech the *Lord*, therefore, to send out laborers to the harvest."
> He said, "O *Lord*, there are *many* around the drinking trough,
> but there is nothing in the cistern."
> Jesus said, "*Many* are standing at the door, but it is the solitary who
> will enter the bridal chamber."

The word-linkage italicized between those sayings is typical of the *Gospel of Thomas* and it represents the most minimal form of written composition. There are also, however, small formal clusters of parables. Three parables concern "a man" in 63–64–65 and three more tell what "The Kingdom of the Father is like" in 96–97–98.

As we shall see in the next section, it is inadvisable to judge

27

this somewhat random assemblage as a sign of literary incompetence. It may just as well be indicative of a particular theological vision.

Theological Vision

Gnosticism. Was gnosticism a Christian heresy, a Jewish heresy, or an original ideology or religion that arose independently of either of them but eventually coalesced powerfully with both of them?

The first option is what one would presume from reading the early patristic attacks on gnosticism and it is a fair expression of their own interests and concerns. Those writers were interested in it exclusively as a Christian heresy. But in the light of the Nag Hammadi Library that explanation of origin is no longer tenable. George MacRae highlighted some of the evidence of pre-Christian gnosticism there discovered and concluded that, "for a growing number of scholars now clearly in the majority, such evidence as just observed regarding certain Nag Hammadi tractates enables us to rule out one of the oldest and most enduring options, namely that Gnosticism is to be seen as heretical offshoot from Christianity" (149).

What of the second option, gnosticism as originally a Jewish heresy, in the light of Nag Hammadi? George MacRae gives his own position quite emphatically,

> For my part, I believe that Gnosticism arose as a revolutionary reaction in Hellenized Judaism wisdom and apocalyptic circles. It became a rival of Christianity not only in the second century when the ecclesiastical writers such as Justin and Irenaeus identified Gnostic leaders and sects, but from the very beginnings of Christian reflection on the significance and message of Jesus. What made the rivalry the more acute—and paradoxically the more influential in shaping the formulations of some early Christians—was the natural affinity arising from a certain common parentage. The Gnosticism of the Nag Hammadi documents is not a Christian heresy but if anything a Jewish heresy, just as primitive Christianity itself should be regarded as a Jewish heresy or set of Jewish heresies (1978:150).

On the other hand, Robert McL. Wilson maintains that, "The Jewish contribution is unmistakable, but whether the whole movement originated within Judaism is quite another matter" (296).

The third option, gnosticism as an originally independent ideology or religion, is my own working hypothesis. Here are definitions of this phenomenon from the two most important books written on the subject within the last fifty years. In his superb study of gnosticism Hans Jonas claimed that "the cardinal feature of gnostic thought is the radical dualism that governs the relation of God and the world, and correspondingly that of man and the world. The deity is absolutely transmundane, its nature alien to that of the universe, which it neither created nor governs and to which it is the complete antithesis: to the divine realm of light, self-contained and remote, the cosmos is opposed as the realm of darkness. The world is the work of lowly powers which though they may be mediately descended from Him do not know the true God and obstruct the knowledge of Him in the cosmos over which they rule" (42). There is a similar emphasis on dualism in the definition proposed recently by Kurt Rudolph. He admits that "a clear-cut definition of this 'religion of knowledge' or of 'insight,' as the Greek word *gnosis* may be translated, is not easy, but ... we shall not go far wrong to see in it a dualistic religion, consisting of several schools and movements, which took up a definitely negative attitude towards the world and the society of the time, and proclaimed a deliverance ('redemption') of man precisely from the constraints of earthly existence through 'insight' into his essential relationship, whether as 'soul' or 'spirit,'—a relationship temporarily obscured—with the supramundane realm of freedom and of rest" (2). In considering gnosticism that radical dualism is more important than cosmological speculation where "we meet with the kind of emphatic and pathetic verbosity which the 'ineffable' seems to have incited in many of its professors" (Jonas: 199).

Asceticism. There are certainly tractates in the Nag Hammadi collection which evince that emphatic and pathetic verbosity and are as Gnostic as anything one could ever desire. But the deliberately assembled collection also contains, for example, a small section of Plato's *Republic* in Codex VI (*NHLE:* 290–91), the *Teachings of Silvanus* in Codex VII (*NHLE:* 346–61), and the *Sentences of Sextus* in Codex XII (*NHLE:* 454–59), and these are just as certainly not Gnostic. Every text in the Nag Hammadi Library can, of course, be read from a Gnostic viewpoint, but then one wonders what text might not be so read. When texts such as the above three are gathered and covered together with texts of full-blown Gnostic speculation, the unity of concern seems to be, not gnosticism, but asceticism. Thus Frederick Wisse has concluded that,

> if there is a unity at all in the Library it must be found not in doctrine but in the ethical stance of the tractates. Particularly the non-Gnostic and marginally Gnostic tractates preach an ascetic morality. God and the pious believer are contrasted to the rest of mankind with their lusts and concerns of the flesh. It is a morality of the elite, the chosen few, who order their lives according to the divine principle within them. Sexuality and womanhood are singled out as the epitome of evil—a tendency of those who live in a monastic or semi-monastic, male society. All indications are that in this esoteric, encratic morality we have a dominant interest of the owners of the Library, one which influenced their choice of holy books and the way they interpreted them (1971:220–21).

Those who unified the Nag Hammadi Library were certainly ascetics and gnostics but some of the works they treasured were ascetic rather than Gnostic. One might argue that asceticism is just practical gnosticism, the gnosticism of those disinterested in theory and speculation. But it does not seem to me that either virginal celibacy, celibate asceticism, or ascetic monasticism is *necessarily* so radically dualistic that the divine, the cosmic, the social, and the human are split into essentially antithetical and warring parts. The presence of such radical and Gnostic dualism will not be proved by practice but by theory, not by action but by vision. All of this background must be kept in mind in considering the *Gospel of Thomas*.

Gospel of Thomas. Where exactly does this gospel fit in that spectrum of asceticism and gnosticism?

Articles, books, and theses have argued that the *Gospel of Thomas* is thorougly and completely Gnostic and other articles, books, and theses have argued a completely opposite position. It seems to me that the gospel is primarily concerned with asceticism rather than gnosticism and while such a document could easily be read within gnosticism or even drawn more and more deeply into its sphere, in itself it still stands on the borders between Catholic and Gnostic Christianity. No doubt the future would not allow any document to remain long in that ambiguous position but that same future would also absorb and retain celibate and ascetic monasticism within Catholic Christianity. It would be the theory rather than the practice that would distinguish Gnostic from Catholic celibacy and the *Gospel of Thomas* can be read with more or less equal plausibility in either theoretical direction.

There are three major emphases in the theological vision of this document but it is only fair to say that theoretical consistency and ideological acuity are not among its primary interests.

1) Wisdom Speculation. Of wisdom it was said in Prov 8:22–23 that, "The Lord created me at the beginning of his work, the first of his acts of old. Ages ago I was set up, at the first, before the beginning of the earth." And again in Sir 24:9, "From eternity, in the beginning, he created me, and for eternity I shall not cease to exist." Finally, in Wis 7:26, "she is a reflection of eternal light, a spotless mirror of the working of God, and an image of his goodness." Take, then, those linked themes of creation, wisdom, light, and image, read Genesis 1 against their background, and a full speculative wisdom theology becomes possible. And what had already happened in Jewish wisdom thinking could easily be transferred to Jesus and the believer in

early Christianity. First, with regard to Jesus. Gen 1:3 starts with, "God said, 'Let there be light'; and there was light." Jesus, accordingly, announces himself as wisdom-light, for example, "It is I who am the light which is above them all" in *Gos. Thom.* 77a. That is only one example of the many sayings throughout *Thomas* in which Jesus speaks in the solemn "I am" announcements traditional for wisdom herself. And since Jesus is divine wisdom, *Thomas* either does not know or does not need any of those other titles used for Jesus elsewhere in early Christianity, for example, Christ, Lord, Savior, Son of David, Son of Man, Son of God. Second, with regard to the believer, Gen 1:26–27 concludes with, "God said, 'Let us make man in our image, after our likeness'; . . . So God created man in his own image, in the image of God he created him; male and female he created them." This combination of primordial light and creational image is connected to the believer in *Gos. Thom.* 50 and 83–84–85. While those sayings are not exactly models of clarity, the opening of *Gos. Thom.* 50 is explicit enough, "If they say to you, 'Where did you come from?,' say to them, 'We came from the light.'" In the summary statement of Stevan L. Davies, whose book may well be the best yet written on the theology of *Thomas*, "In both Qumran and Wisdom literature Wisdom and light are equivalent terms. It is Thomas' peculiar trait to equate Kingdom with light and to use Kingdom in place of the term Wisdom" (56).

2) Paradise Regained. This second aspect flows directly from the first one. *Thomas* is polemically anti-apocalyptic. This aspect of its theology is sometimes called realized eschatology which implies that it looks to the future, to the last things, and believes that they are already present and available to the believer here below. I do not think that is the best way to describe a vision where the first things have returned rather than the last things are present. *Thomas* is enthralled not by the arrival of the end but by the return of the beginning. Its vision is of paradise regained. Davies has noted that "Thomas contains a

32

variety of logia which are in the form of questions and answers, questions by the disciples as a group and answers by Jesus. The questions predominantly are about the time of the end or about the nature of Jesus. In both cases the disciples' questions seem to indicate their failure to understand" (82–83). Corrections about the end of time appear in *Gos. Thom.* 18, 51, 113 and corrections about the nature of Jesus appear in *Gos. Thom.* 24, 37, 43, 52, 91. Both sets of corrections coalesce to say that what they seek is already before their eyes if they can but see it. The polemical overtones of those corrections are also quite evident, in fact derisively so, in *Gos. Thom.* 3, "If those who lead you say to you, 'See, the Kingdom is in the sky,' then the birds of the sky will precede you. If they say to you, 'It is in the sea,' then the fish will precede you. Rather, the Kingdom is inside of you, and it is outside of you." The Kingdom is, like wisdom, both inside and outside the believer, both an internal gift and a cosmic presence. And, as Davies reminds us, "the use of Kingdom for Wisdom is certainly not a feature of traditional Jewish Wisdom literature; it is a new move, a creative shift of the tradition" (45). But *Thomas* does not so much think of the future as already present as it thinks of the past as still available. Thus in *Gos. Thom.* 18, "The disciples said to Jesus, 'Tell us how our end will be.' Jesus said, 'Have you discovered, then, the beginning, that you look for the end. For where the beginning is, there will the end be. Blessed is he who will take his place in the beginning; he will know the end and will not experience death.'"

3) Sexual Asceticism. This third major theme flows directly from that second one. Here is paradise regained in practice. In *Gos. Thom.* 4, 11, 16, 22, 23, 49, 75, 106 there are a series of sayings extolling the "single one" or the "solitary." This derives from Jewish speculation on the androgynous nature of Adam before he was split into Adam and Eve. A. F. J. Klijn explains *Thomas'* meaning as follows: "(a) The word 'single one' is equivalent to the elect and saved ones. (b) Originally man was a 'single one,' but he became 'two.' In order to be saved he has to

become a 'single one' again. This means that he has to return to his original state. (c) The original 'single one' has become 'two' by becoming male and female. As a result we may say that the Gospel of Thomas speaks about salvation as a return to the original state and that it rejects the division of man into male and female" (272). The practical result of this vision is, of course, celibate and preferably virginal existence. You can see this stated neutrally in *Gos. Thom.* 22, "When you make the male and the female one and the same, so that the male not be male nor the female female ... then will you enter [the Kingdom]." And you can see it stated with ineffable chauvinism in *Gos. Thom.* 114, "For every woman who will make herself male will enter the Kingdom of Heaven." In the light of this sexual asceticism, the somewhat cavalier rejection of normal Jewish piety found in *Gos. Thom.* 6a+14 or 104 may indicate not so much liberalism as an insistence on the inadequacy of such minor ascetical practices. What *Thomas* demands is not some periodical fasting from food but a permanent fasting from sex, as in *Gos. Thom.* 27, "If you do not fast as regards the world, you will not find the Kingdom." In all of this, *Thomas* is profoundly basic to the traditions of sexual asceticism in eastern Syria just as later it would fit well within the Pachomian monastic movement in Upper Egypt.

When all those traits are brought together in a gospel of wisdom's utterances, *Thomas* may well have considered that any one saying is as powerful as any other, that compositional order or climax is not pertinent, that the narrative is not in the gospel but in the gospel's reception, and that the unorder given to the gospel is just perfect for its subject. The *Gospel of Thomas* is what Jewish wisdom theology looks like after it has heard Jesus' message about the Kingdom of God.

In summary, then, the *Gospel of Thomas* is precisely on the ambiguous borderline between Gnostic and Catholic Christianity. As such it could be read and then pulled in either direction. Its later Gnostic usage can be seen in the *Acts of*

Thomas (*NTA:* 1.287) and in Manicheism (*NTA:* 1.283). But, unfortunately, Catholic Christianity never produced some pseudepigraphical "Epistles of Thomas," letters of therapeutic interpretation which might have redeemed the *Gospel of Thomas* from such as the *Acts of Thomas,* just as the Pastoral Epistles redeemed Paul from such as the *Acts of Paul* and the Johannine Epistles redeemed John from such as the *Acts of John.*

INDEPENDENCE

In the preceding section scholarship was divided on the presence of gnosticism in the *Gospel of Thomas.* It is similarly divided on the relationship between this gospel and the four intracanonical ones. Is it a dependent collection of sayings from within those four gospels or is it an indpendent witness to the tradition about the sayings of Jesus? Two separate reasons persuade me that *Thomas* is completely independent of the intracanonical tradition but I would emphasize that independent does not necessarily mean earlier and earlier does not necessarily mean better.

Order. In a 1979 article B. de Solages drew up in columns the sequential units in the *Gospel of Thomas* and their parallels in the four intracanonical gospels. The lines drawn from one column to another presented a veritable spider's web and showed absolutely no traces of common order between *Thomas* and any of the others. Remember two points. First, *Thomas* itself has no compositional order or sequence and would therefore have had no reason to reorder the sequence of sayings borrowed from those other gospels. Second, if you think of those others as they were written without any chapter and verse distinctions and in margin-to-margin capitals, it would probably be impossible to copy sayings without some copying of order as well. One example may suffice. *Gos. Thom.* 33 reads: "Jesus said, 'Preach from your housetops that which you will hear in your ear {(and) in the other ear}. For no one lights a lamp and puts it under a bushel, nor does he put it in a hidden place, but rather he sets it on a lampstand so that everyone who enters and leaves will see its light.'" That first part in 33a on *Open Proclamation* is found by itself in Matt 10:27 = Luke 12:3 and that second part in 33b on the *Lamp and Bushel* is found by itself in both Mark 4:21 = Luke 8:16 and Matt 5:15 = Luke 11:33.

Content. Here, unfortunately, as controversy came in the door methodology went out the window. There is little real profit in comparing the content of a unit in *Thomas* and its parallel within one of the intracanonical gospels, and then arguing which came from which. Any decent exegete should be able to furnish several reasons in either direction on demand. Proper methodology has three steps. First, one must make a prior separation of what is traditionally present from what is redactionally personal within the intracanonical gospel. Second, if the former is also found in *Thomas*, one can only conclude that they both share common tradition and that, of course, is not at all unexpected. But if the latter is found in *Thomas*, one has a very strong argument for its dependence on the intracanonical writing involved. For how could precisely what is redactional and editorial, personal and individual within one text be found outside of it in another text except by copying? Third, and unfortunately, the opposite is not necessarily true. If redactional elements are absent from *Thomas*, one might still claim dependence by arguing that *Thomas* disagreed with and hence removed all such redactional motifs. This is not pure special pleading since it is indeed hypothetically possible. For instance, Matthew and Luke often remove Markan redactional traits as they rewrite him into their own gospels. However, one should then be able to explain in precise detail why each item was omitted. This proper methodology was used by John H. Sieber in his 1966 dissertation at the Claremont Graduate School in California and he concluded "that there is very little redactional evidence, if any, for holding that our Synoptic Gospels were the sources of Thomas' synoptic sayings. In the great majority of sayings there is no such evidence at all" (262). One example may again suffice. The first beatitude in Luke 6:20b has "Blessed are you poor, for yours is the kingdom of God," but in Matt 5:3, "Blessed are the poor in spirit, for theirs is the kingdom of heaven." Scholars had long considered that "in spirit" was a personal, redactional addition by Matthew himself. Now in *Gos. Thom.* 54 we have, "Blessed are the poor, for yours is the Kingdom of Heaven." Precisely what is missing is the proposed editorial addition of Matthew. But what if one objects that *Thomas* has simply copied Luke here? That will not work. One would have at least to argue that *Thomas* (a) took the third person "the poor" from Matthew, then (b) the second person "yours" from Luke, and (c) returned to Matthew for the final "Kingdom of Heaven." It might be simpler to suggest that Thomas was mentally unstable.

Those two reasons convince me that the tradition in *Thomas* is independent of the intracanonical gospels but, of course, this working hypothesis will have to be tested in every single case to be considered. It also seems to me that the following judgment by George MacRae is quite correct: "It now appears that a majority of scholars who have seriously investigated the matter have been won over to the side of 'Thomas" independence of the canonical Gospels, though these scholars hold a variety of views about the actual history of the composition of 'the Gospel of Thomas'" (1978:152).

2 CASE STUDY 1
THE GREAT SUPPER

The first case study involves a parable, *The Great Supper*, which is extant in three versions, one in the extracanonical *Gos. Thom.* 64, and two in the intracanonical Matt 22:1–14 and Luke 14:16–24. I shall consider then separately rather than simultaneously but develop the comparisons between them as I proceed.

THE PARABLE IN GOS. THOM. 64
Context

As noted earlier, *Thomas* created small formal clusters of three parables in 63–64–65 and 96–97–98. The present parable, then, is in the center of that former triad. All three of its parables conclude with aphorisms. *Gos. Thom.* 63 and 65 have "Let him who has ears hear," and 64 has "Businessmen and merchants will not enter the Places of My Father." This deliberate framing in external format draws attention to a similar coincidence in internal content. Before, then, we even read the parable of *The Great Supper* in 64, we are in a general context of warning against the pernicious effects of worldly concern and monetary concentration.

Text

There are three main narrative elements in the parable as told in *Gos. Thom.* 64: *Situation, Former Guests, Latter Guests.*

Situation. The translation by Lambdin reads "A man had received visitors. And when he had prepared the dinner, he sent his servant to invite the guests" (*NHLE:* 125). This seems to envisage a situation where the arrival of unexpected visitors

39

necessitates the sudden arrangement of a dinner for their enter-
tainment and thus the unwarned invitation of others. Since,
however, the same Coptic word is used for "visitors" and
"guests," it seems better to adopt a simpler translation: "A man
had guests, and when he had prepared the dinner, he sent his
servant to invite the guests." But in any case, one immediately
senses a possible problem. In *Thomas'* version there is no forewarning of the banquet. It is as if you or I decided on a Saturday
morning to have a party that very evening and, with preparations fully underway, started to phone around to various
friends. Also, there is only a single servant involved, so that he
will have to make the complete circuit of all the proposed
guests before he can report back on any one of them.

Former Guests.　　There are four guests contacted by the servant and I shall line out the dialogue in detail:

A. First Guest:
   (1) "He went to the first one and said to him, 'My master invites
       you.'
   (2) He said, 'I have claims against some merchants.
   (3) They are coming to me this evening.
   (4) I must go and give them my orders.
   (5) I ask to be excused from the dinner.'"
B. Second Guest:
   (1) "He went to another and said to him, 'My master has invited
       you.'
   (2) He said to him, 'I have just bought a house
   (3) and am required for the day.
   (4) I shall not have any spare time.'"
C. Third Guest:
   (1) "He went to another and said to him, 'My master invites you.'
   (2) He said to him, 'My friend is going to get married,
   (3) and I am to prepare the banquet.
   (4) I shall not be able to come.
   (5) I ask to be excused from the dinner.'"
D. Fourth Guest:
   (1) "He went to another and said to him, 'My master invites you.'
   (2) He said to him, 'I have just bought a farm,

(3) and I am on my way to collect the rent.
(4) I shall not be able to come.
(5) I ask to be excused.'"

There are three points to be made about the narrative element concerning the *Former Guests*.

1) Four Guests. In a classic article of 1909 Axel Olrik cited the "Law of Three" among his laws or conventions of folk narrative. He noted that "three is the maximum number of men and objects which occur in traditional narrative. Nothing distinguishes the great bulk of folk narrative from modern literature and from reality as much as does the number three" (133). And he concluded that, "the Law of Three extends like a broad swath cut through the world of folk tradition, through the centuries and millenia of human culture. The Semitic, and even more, the Aryan culture, is subject to this dominant force. The beginnings of its rule are, in spite of all the recent excavations and discoveries, lost in the obscurity of prehistory" (134). Jesus' parables usually stay clearly within this triadic convention. Think, for example, of the three servants in *The Talents* of Matt 25:14–28, and the path, rocky ground, thorns in *The Sower* of Mark 4:3–8, or the Priest, Levite, Samaritan in *The Good Samaritan* of Luke 10:30–35. One expects, therefore, triple rather than quadruple phenomena in his parables. This renders surprising the presence of four rather than three guests in *Thomas* and it raises the possibility that an original three may have been expanded to four for redactional purposes by *Thomas*.

2) Commercial Emphasis. In terms of form, one of the above four dialogues between servant and guest is doubly different from the others. B1, the invitation, has "My master has invited you" whereas A1, C1, D1 all have "My master invites you." And B5, the apology, is absent from that dialogue although it is present in A5, C5, D5, "I ask to be excused (from the dinner)." I propose, therefore, that the second guest has been added by *Thomas* to turn an original threesome into the present foursome. The reason why this was done may be seen in terms of

content. The original triad of excuses involved claims against some merchants, preparing a friend's wedding banquet, collecting a farm's rent. That means only two out of three reasons involved commercial transactions. Thomas intended to heighten the commercial emphasis of the parable so he added a new excuse as B2, "I have just bought a house," on the analogy of D2, "I have just bought a farm." Thus three out of four excuses now pertain to business transactions.

3) Direct Discourse. The dialogues between servant and guests are recorded in direct speech. This means that we can actually hear their excuses for ourselves and we can hear that they are quite detailed, very reasonable, and extremely polite: "I pray to be excused." The master, having called a dinner without warning, finds that each of his proposed guests has a perfectly valid reason why he cannot come on that specific evening. All takes place within the rubrics of the possible and the plausible.

Latter Guests. Next comes the third element in the parable's narrative. Once again we are in direct discourse, but now between master and servant: "The servant returned and said to his master, 'Those whom you invited to the dinner have asked to be excused.' The master said to his servant, 'Go outside to the streets and bring back those whom you happen to meet, so that they may dine.'" With all the expected and invited guests unavailable, the master simply fills the dinner at random with the unexpected and the uninvited, not with his friends but with strangers.

Interpretation

The meaning of the parable is quite clear for *Thomas*. It is interpreted externally and contextually by its insertion within the parabolic triad of *Gos. Thom.* 63–64–65 all of which warn against worldly interests and commercial concerns. It is interpreted internally and textually both by the addition of a fourth excuse (B) to the original three excuses (A, C, D), and also by the concluding aphorism, "Businessmen and merchants will not enter the Places of My Father." This is not the master of the dinner speaking but Jesus himself. And this represents the only time that *Thomas* appends an interpretation to a parable. This special addition to the central parable of the triad may have been intended to reflect interpretation on all three stories in *Gos. Thom.* 63–64–65.

THE PARABLE IN LUKE 14:16–24

Context

Luke 14:1–14 has grouped a series of Jesus' sayings concerning meal situations within an actual meal situation itself. There are four units involved and each one opens with a reminder of the symposium situation. First, in 14:1–6, there is a healing "one sabbath when he went to dine at the house of a ruler who belonged to the Pharisees." Second, in 14:7–11, he speaks of places of honor "to those who were invited." Third, in 14:12–14, "He said also to the man who had invited him, 'When you give a dinner or a banquet, do not invite your friends or your brothers or your kinsmen or rich neighbors, lest they also invite you in return, and you be repaid. But when you give a feast, invite the poor, the maimed, the lame, the blind, and you will be blessed, because they cannot repay you. You will be repaid at the resurrection of the just." Fourth, in 14:15–24, the parable of *The Great Supper* is introduced by this dialogue: "When one of those who sat at table with him heard this, he said to him, 'Blessed is he who shall eat bread in the kingdom of God.'"

Text

There are four narrative elements in the Lukan version of the parable: *Situation, Former Guests, Host's Reaction, Latter Guests.* There was no equivalent to that third element in *Thomas'* version.

Situation. Luke 14:16–17 begins the parable with, "A man once gave a great banquet, and invited many; and at the time for the banquet he sent his servant to say to those who had been invited, 'Come; for all is now ready.'" There are two important differences from *Thomas'* opening. First, the meal has escalated from a dinner with three or four guests to a "great banquet" with "many" guests invited. Second, the culpability of the guests, which was totally absent in *Thomas*, is now quite evident, since they have been forewarned and had presumably accepted the invitation. In other words, the dinner is no longer an unexpected situation. Actually, however, both those elements cause tensions within the Lukan version. Later on in the story, when we get to the former guests, we shall find that there are only three of them mentioned and that they are just as polite as in *Thomas*.

Former Guests. Luke 14:18–20 does not have a complete direct discourse dialogue for each guest but he begins with, "But they all alike began to make excuses," and then gives the three excuses in direct speech. I shall number the parts as corresponding to those in *Thomas:*

A. First Guest:
   (2) "The first said to him, 'I have bought a field,
   (3) and I must go out and see it;
   (5) I pray you, have me excused.'"
B. Second Guest:
   (2) "And another said, 'I have bought five yoke of oxen,
   (3) and I go to examine them;
   (5) I pray you, have me excused.'"
C. Third Guest:
   (2) "And another said, 'I have married a wife,
   (4) and therefore I cannot come.'"

One notices immediately that the guests here are the conventional triad. The excuses are no longer four-part responses, as in *Thomas*, but only three-part ones, and yet, as I have indicated by the numbers above, a full four-part process can still be discerned across the three excuses, and it is very similar to that in *Thomas:* (2) I have bought, (3) I must go, (4) I cannot come, (5)

I ask to be excused. Once again, the excuses are plausible and possible, realistic and polite. But in Luke, since they have been forewarned of the banquet, one almost feels that their politeness is hypocritical and simply adds to their guilt. Also, when you note how the form of the third excuse differs from that of the first and second ones in Luke, you might well wonder if Luke adapted the original third one to its present form. It is probably Luke himself who wanted to include a "wife" among those occupations distracting from the heavenly banquet, just as Luke 18:29 adds "wife" to the list of family members to be abandoned in Mark 10:29 = Matt 19:29. This is similar to the telltale change in form that indicated a new content in *Thomas'* second guest.

Host's Reaction. This is a new element, not found in *Thomas*, and it is mentioned but almost in passing and within the next element concerning the *Latter Guests*. It notes that "the householder in anger said" and this anger is now quite understandable since the guests had been warned beforehand about the banquet and were now simply being told that all was ready.

Latter Guests. Luke 14:21–24 contains the most interesting development of all so far: "So the servant came and reported this to his master. Then the householder in anger said to his servant, 'Go out quickly to the streets and lanes of the city, and bring in the poor and maimed and blind and lame.' And the servant said, 'Sir, what you commanded has been done, and still there is room.' And the master said to the servant, 'Go out to the highways and hedges, and compel people to come in, that my house may be filled. For I tell you, none of those men who were invited shall taste my banquet.'" There are two very significant changes here. First, there are two sendings for the *Latter Guests*, one to the city and one to the country. Second, the four categories of suffering from the context in Luke 14:13, "the poor, the maimed, the lame, the blind," are now introduced into the text at Luke 14:21, "the poor and maimed and blind and lame."

45

Interpretation

The double sending for the *Latter Guests* is best seen as a factor in Luke's interpretation of the parable. He reads the story, not just as a general warning like *Thomas*, but as a specific allegorical description of early Christianity's relationship to Judaism, that is, as the opening dialogue puts it, of those "who shall eat bread in the kingdom of God" (Luke 14:15). In Luke's interpretation those who refused to come to the banquet would be "the lawyers and Pharisees" among whom Jesus is sitting and to whom he is speaking, see 14:1–2 and 14:15. They are replaced, first, by the suffering outcasts of Israel from "the streets and lanes of the city," and, second, by believing Gentiles, that is, by those farther away, from "the highways and hedges." If ascetic morality dominates *Thomas'* reading, historical allegory dominates Luke's interpretation.

What is especially significant here is how later events, the events of early Christian history as seen by Luke, have inserted themselves into the text of the past parable of Jesus. The words of Jesus which shaped those events have become themselves shaped by that which they originated. Text and event have created one another in an interpretative interplay, a hermeneutical dance.

THE PARABLE IN MATT 22:1–14

Context

Just as the context of Luke 14:12–14 has profoundly changed the Lukan parable of 14:16–24, so also has the context of Matt 21:33–44 even more profoundly changed the Matthean parable in 22:1–14.

What Matthew did was to form a parabolic diptych of two stories, first, *The Wicked Tenants,* concerning an owner and his tenants in 21:33–44, and second, *The Great Supper,* concerning a king and his guests in 22:1–14. He then placed as their interpretive hinge this statement in 21:45–46: "When the chief priests and the Pharisees heard his parables, they perceived that he was speaking about them. But when they tried to arrest him, they feared the multitudes, because they held him to be a prophet." Within this diptych context, the lethal violence of the former parable has infiltrated the originally pacific situation of the latter one. For example, in the parable of *The Wicked Tenants*, instead of the single servant of Mark and Luke, the owner "sent his servants" and "again he sent other servants" in Matt 21:34, 46; so also in that of *The Great Supper*, instead of the single servant of *Thomas* and Luke, the king "sent his servants" and "again he sent other servants" in Matt 22:3, 4. And just as servants were "killed" in the first parable at Matt 21:36, so also were they "killed" in the second parable at Matt 22:6. Thus, the context of parabolic diptych is quite clear in Matthew 21–22.

Text

Instead of three in *Thomas* and four in Luke, there are now five narrative elements in Matthew's version of the parable: *Situation, Former Guests, Host's Reaction, Latter Guests, Wedding Garment*.

Situation. This is given in Matt 22:2–3a with, "The kingdom of heaven may be compared to a king who gave a marriage feast for his son and sent his servants to call those who were invited to the marriage feast." First, the escalation of situation continues: from a "dinner" in *Thomas*, to a "great banquet" in Luke, to a wedding feast for a royal heir in Matthew. Second, there is again forewarning, as in Luke but not in *Thomas*, and, of course, the royal occasion renders belated refusal much more serious. Third, the messengers are now appropriately plural.

Former Guests. Next follows the refusal of the first set of guests in 22:3b–6, "But they would not come. Again he sent other servants, saying, 'Tell those who were invited, Behold I have made ready my dinner, my oxen and my fat calves are killed, and everything is ready; come to the marriage feast.' But

47

they made light of it and went off, one to his farm, another to his business, while the rest seized his servants, treated them shamefully, and killed them." This is clearly a very different case from either *Thomas* or Luke. First, there are twin sendings of plural servants for the *Former Guests* in Matthew just as there were twin sendings of a single servant for the *Latter Guests* in Luke. Second, we have no direct dialogue but hear only the voice of the king himself, "Behold, I have made ready . . . come." Third, instead of politely plausible excuses, there is now abuse and murder.

Host's Reaction. After such a lethal response, one is not surprised that the element of *Host's Response*, absent entirely from *Thomas*, cited simply as anger and in passing in Luke, is now fully developed in Matt 22:7, "The king was angry, and he sent his troops and destroyed those murderers and burned their city." This has now become a full and separate element in the story's sequence.

Latter Guests. This is in Matt 22:8-10, "Then he said to his servants, 'The wedding is ready, but those invited were not worthy. Go therefore to the thoroughfares, and invite to the marriage feast as many as you find.' And those servants went out into the streets and gathered all whom they found, both bad and good; so the wedding hall was filled with guests." Like *Thomas*, but unlike Luke, Matthew has only one sending here, but the new guests are specified as "both bad and good." There is, of course, nothing whatsoever about Luke's own particular mention of "the poor and maimed and blind and lame."

Wedding Garment. Finally, in Matt 22:11-14, there is a new narrative element, one which had no parallel in either *Thomas* or Luke. "But when the king came in to look at the guests, he saw there a man who had no wedding garment; and he said to him, 'Friend, how did you get in here without a wedding garment?' And he was speechless. Then the king said to the attendants, 'Bind him hand and foot, and cast him into the outer darkness; there men will weep and gnash their teeth.' For many are called, but few are chosen." I consider that all of this is Matthew's own composition, a creative addition to interpret the parable according to his own particular vision of its meaning. Its three sections may be considered separately.

1) Matt 22:11–12. You will recall that, while *Thomas* and Luke allowed direct discourse on the lips of servant, guests, and host, Matt 22:4, 8 had allowed direct discourse only on the lips of the king himself. This same procedure is found in 22:12 so that it follows Mattthew's own pattern for the story.

2) Matt 22:13. This is one of Matthew's own dearly loved phrases, and, in full panoply, it has three parts: (a) bound hand and foot, (b) cast into outer darkness, (c) there men will weep and gnash their teeth. Matthew has that third part in Matt 13:42, 50, and he has added it on to Matt 24:51 = Luke 12:46. He has also added on the second and third parts to Matt 8:11–12 = Luke 13:28–29 and Matt 25:29–30 = Luke 19:26–27. Finally, here in Matt 22:13 he has all three parts of the phrase. Put simply, Matt 22:13 is pure and vintage Matthew.

3) Matt 22:14. This is not a statement of the king within the narrative frames of the parable but an aphorism placed on the lips of Jesus to serve as a concluding comment on all of 22:1–13. The saying is independently known from the anonymous treatise traditionally called the *Epistle of Barnabas*, which dates from the early thirties of the second century. This work, which employs an allegorical interpretation of the Old Testament in the tradition of Philo of Alexandria, warns at *Barn.* 4:14, "And consider this also, my brethren, when you see that after such great signs and wonders were wrought in Israel they were even then finally abandoned;—let us take heed lest as it was written we be found 'many called but few chosen.'"

I conclude, therefore, that all of Matt 22:11–14 is due to Matthew's own creative reading of Jesus' parable. He himself composed the dialogue between king and guest and the condemnation which concluded it. And he then appended the traditional aphorism to terminate the entire unit.

Interpretation

For Luke the parable was an allegory of Christian history but with an emphasis on the outcasts of Israel and the Gentiles who received the replacement invitation. For Matthew the parable is also an allegory of Christian history but in a much more detailed fashion and with the emphasis now on the past punishment of those who refused the first invitation and the future punishment of those who were inadequate for the replacement invitation. Here is how Matthew reads the parable. God has invited his people, has twice invited them, possibly through the prophets of old and the apostles more recently, to come to the marriage feast for Jesus. They have lethally refused, in Matthew's view, and the destruction of "their city," presumably of Jerusalem by Titus in 70 A.D., was their punishment. Now the Gentiles have taken their place at the feast. But, and this is characteristically Matthean, even among those actually at the feast, there are "both good and bad." On the last day, at the final judgment, God will review the guests and then it will not be enough simply to be at the feast, it will be necessary to be properly attired as well. Matthew, in other words, knows certain members in the church whose ultimate fate he does not consider to be eternal happiness. Possibly their attitude towards the Mosaic Law was one of which he disapproved. So also, in the preceding parable of *The Wicked Tenants*, the new tenants who replaced the old ones must make certain to "give him the fruits in their seasons" in Matt 21:41. And in an earlier parable, recorded in Matt 13:24–30 and *Gos. Thom.* 57, but interpreted only in Matt 13:36–43, Matthew knows that there are both wheat and weeds in the kingdom, but "at the close of the age," in the last judgment, "the Son of man will send his angels, and they will gather out of his kingdom all causes of sin and all evildoers, and throw them into the furnace of fire; there men will weep and gnash their teeth" (13:40–41).

Once again history has infiltrated the parable that created it.

Text and event intertwine but now the event is as Matthew sees it and not as Luke sees it and so their parables differ profoundly not only in detail but in emphasis, not only in emphasis but in sweep and vision.

THE PARABLE IN TRADITION
Transmission

It is now possible to summarize that preceding transmissional analysis over four main stages.

First, there is the parable of Jesus. Since Jesus was an oral poet it may be presumed that, if he told the same parable on several occasions, the details would expand and contract to suit and fit the time, place, and audience available. This is the way of the oral story-teller. At the moment, for instance, it takes about a minute to read the parable of *The Good Samaritan*. For Jesus to have told it may have taken an hour. And if he told it more than once, it might have taken one hour the first time and three the second. That also is the way of the oral story-teller. But the structural outline or plot summary would have remained steady and it is such plot summaries that the tradition retained, transmitted, and interpreted. In the case of *The Great Supper*, then, that inaugural plot summary involved an ordinary situation when a host decides on a sudden dinner and by the time his servant returns with the news that none of his friends is available he has everything ready and so brings in anyone he can find. It is a perfectly plausible everyday possibility but it results in a most paradoxical vision: all the expected guests are absent and only unexpected guests are present. The Kingdom of God, says Jesus, is like that paradoxical image. The parable stands, then, to challenge the tradition it had created and to create the tradition it had challenged. Who do you think, it asks, are the insiders who are out and the outsiders who are in? It should be noted that the hermeneutics of the parable will involve not only external and contextual commentary but also and especially internal and textual retelling, that is, variations on the general narrative structure, modulations on the basic plot summary.

Second, for *Thomas* the insiders who are out are those involved in commercial activities and the outsiders who are in are those who have ascetically withdrawn from all such worldly pursuits.

Third, for Luke the insiders who are out are the authorities of Israel, the outsiders who are in are both the outcasts of Israel and the believing Gentiles.

Fourth, for Matthew the insiders who are out are again the authorities of Israel, and the outsiders who are in are believers, presumably both Jews and Gentiles. But now there is a second discriminant. It is not enough for those outsiders simply to be in, they must also be properly attired. Thus the parable's paradoxical core is turned not only outwards against Judaism but now inwards against Christianity itself.

It is clear, I hope, that the multiplicity and diversity of interpretation does not bespeak the tradition's failure but the parable's success. Its function was to generate response and its abiding vitality is maintained only and as long as new interpretations are generated by it. If one wishes univocal statement, one avoids parable. If one chooses parable, one wishes continual interpretation.

Intertextuality

There is one other special aspect of two of those interpretations. In Luke and Matthew, and in characteristically divergent ways, the text of Christian history after Jesus intertwines with the text of the parable itself. That means that the future which came after the parable is now texted within it. The horizons of Jesus' story and of Christian history have merged and in this intertextuality it becomes extremely difficult to be certain where one ends and the other begins. We shall see much more of such intertextuality as we proceed.

3 CASE STUDY 2
THE EVIL TENANTS

That first case involved a parable, this one concerns the intersection of a parable and an aphorism. There are four versions involved: *Gos. Thom.* 65–66; Mark 12:1–11 = Matt 21:33–43[44] = Luke 20:9–18.

PARABLE AND APHORISM IN GOS. THOM. 65–66

Parable in Gos. Thom. 65

The parable of *The Evil Tenants* appears in *Gos. Thom.* 65. The story has three elements, *Vineyard, Messengers, Murder,* and reads as follows: "There was a good man who owned a vineyard. He leased it to tenant farmers so that they might work it and he might collect the produce from them. He sent his servant so that the tenants might give him the produce of the vineyard. They seized his servant and beat him, all but killing him. The servant went back and told his master. The master said, 'Perhaps <they> did not recognize <him>.' He sent another servant. The tenants beat this one as well. Then the owner sent his son and said, 'Perhaps they will show respect to my son.' Because the tenants knew that it was he who was the heir to the vineyard, they seized him and killed him."

The context of this story was reviewed in the last case study and the three parables in *Gos. Thom.* 63–64–65 were seen as a triadic cluster integrated by generic status, opening format, concluding aphorisms, and general interpretation. In itself, then, *Gos. Thom.* 65 is closed off quite clearly by this prior linkage. If one had read only *Thomas*, the parable is, like the two preceding ones, a dire warning against the evil consequences of material greed and needed no more comment that its concluding "Let him who has ears hear." The reader is supposed to be horrified at how material desires lead to murder.

The text has three very interesting features. First, the owner is a "good" man and so fails completely to understand the dangerous and rebellious nature of the situation. Second, the owner speaks twice in direct discourse and these two comments are linguistically balanced by the double "perhaps." As indicated by the diamond brackets in the text, the editor has corrected it from "Perhaps he did not recognize them" to "Perhaps they did not recognize him." In the former reading, the owner thinks the problem is that the servant went to the wrong tenants. In the latter, and much more likely reading, the owner thinks that the tenants will not accept the authority of the servant. In any case, this first comment is extremely important in establishing the possibility of the story's realistic continuance. The owner, being a good man and thinking it was all some misunderstanding, concluded that it would take the authority of his son to get a positive response from the tenants. That is why he was so misguided as to send his son into such a lethal situation. Like the preceding case, this parable is carefully plotted for plausibility. Third, there are three messengers: servant, another servant, and son. And here Jesus follows, as expected, the triadic convention for his parable.

Aphorism in Gos. Thom. 66

The aphorism of *The Rejected Stone* appears in *Gos. Thom.* 66: "Jesus said, "Show me the stone which the builders have rejected. That one is the corner stone.'"

In terms of context, this is separated quite clearly from the preceding parable by the new "Jesus said." If one only had *Thomas*, therefore, one would not imagine any special connection between *Gos. Thom.* 65 and 66.

In terms of text, this places on the lips of Jesus a restatement of Ps 118:22, "The stone which the builders rejected has become the head of the corner." This same Old Testament text was applied to Jesus by Peter in Acts 4:11, "This is the stone which was rejected by you builders, but which has become the head of the corner." It is also applied to Jesus in 1 Pet 2:4–8 where in 2:6 he is *The Precious Stone* from Isa 28:16, in 2:7 he is *The Rejected Stone* from Ps 118:22, and in 2:8 he is *The Stumbling Stone* from Isa 8:14.

But here in *Gos. Thom.* 66 this text is used by Jesus presumably of himself. It is not even clear, however, that *Thomas* wishes to make anything out of the biblical text as prophecy. Recall *Gos. Thom.* 52, "His disciples said to Him, 'Twenty-four prophets spoke in Israel, and all of them spoke in You.' He said to them, 'You have omitted the one living in your presence and have spoken (only) of the dead.'" In any case, the formulation of Ps 118:22 is somewhat changed in *Gos. Thom.* 66.

PARABLE AND APHORISM IN THE SYNOPTICS

Scholars have long recognized some sort of direct literary relationship between the three synoptic gospels, Matthew, Mark, and Luke. Various solutions have been proposed and the one I myself accept and use is called the Two Source solution because it proposes that, apart from other separate sources, Matthew and Luke used two common sources in composing their gospels. One of these common sources is a narrative gospel, Mark, which is still, of course, independently available to us, and the other is termed Q (*Quelle* is German for source), which is no longer independently available but which can be discerned and reconstructed from the order and content of the non-Markan material common to Matthew and Luke. This Two Source theory must achieve operational validity by passing certain internal and external tests. Internally, for example, it must be able to show how every omission or alteration of a Markan text by Matthew or Luke can be explained as part of coherent redactional theologies different from that of their

Markan source. Externally, those redactional theologies must then fit into the wider frames and trajectories of early Christianity. Such tests are never absolute proof but practical confirmation and they can be refuted and replaced only by alternative proposals deemed by one's contemporaries and successors as more valid.

I consider, therefore, that the parable of *The Great Supper* in Matt 22:1-14 and Luke 14:15-24 were both derived but completely redeveloped from Q and that the parable of *The Evil Tenants* derives from Mark 12:1-11 into both Matt 21:33-43[44] and Luke 20:9-18. It must be admitted, however, that in this instance a case can be made for Luke 20:9-18 as a separate and independent version of the parable.

Parable and Aphorism in Mark 12:1-11

The situation of *Gos. Thom.* 65-66 is handled very differently in Mark 12:1-11 where parable and aphorism appear integrated together into a narrative sequence with five elements: *Vineyard, Messengers, Murder, Punishment, Aphorism.*

Vineyard. There was no description of the vineyard in *Thomas* but Mark 12:1 says, "A man planted a vineyard, and set a hedge around it, and dug a pit for the wine press, and built a tower." This is a quite obvious allusion to the Greek Septuagint translation of Isa 5:1-2, "My beloved had a vineyard on a very fertile hill. He digged it and cleared it of stones, and planted it with choice vines; he built a watchtower in the midst of it, and hewed out a wine vat in it; and he looked for it to yield grapes, but it yielded wild grapes." Isaiah's parable speaks only of a vineyard which brings forth bad grapes; there is no question of tenants. But this biblical allusion in Mark 12:1 immediately refers the vineyard to Israel and makes one wonder who, then, are the tenants. It becomes clear by Mark 12:12 that the tenants are the authorities of Israel who know "that he had told the parable against them."

Messengers. In Mark 12:3-5 the owner sends three single

servants, and one is beaten, one wounded, one killed, "and so with many others, some they beat and some they killed." You will recall that, in *Thomas*, there are no murders prior to that of the son and that the owner thinks that the tenants simply will not accept the authority claimed by the servant. Such murderous activities prior to the sending of the son render the father's action implausible and unbelievable within the conventions of a realistic narrative. This serves to underline the careful plausibility of the *Thomas* version.

Murder. In Mark 12:6–7 the son and heir is sent, murdered, and venomously tossed unburied from the vineyard. Once again, however, the earlier murders render pathetic the father's comment "they will respect my son" and render stupid his sending of the heir without support from the forces at his disposal.

Punishment. In Mark 12:9 Jesus asks rhetorically "What will the owner of the vineyard do?" And he then answers his own question with, "He will come and destroy the tenants, and give the vineyard to others." First, the question, even as rhetorical question, breaks the parabolic closure. Second, the tense is changed from past to future. Third, the owner's belated use of force and his decision to go on with the leasing program thereafter does not increase the narrative plausibility. Fourth, there was no punishment element in *Thomas* and there the impotence of an absentee landlord rendered the story coherent and complete. Fifth, this rhetorical question seems another allusion to the vineyard parable from Isaiah. There in 5:4 God rhetorically asks Israel, "What more was there to do for my vineyard, that I had not done in it? When I looked for it to yield grapes, why did it yield wild grapes?"

Aphorism. In Mark 12:10–11 Jesus concludes with the saying of *The Rejected Stone* in Ps 118:22–23. First, the third-person closure of parable is again broken by a second-person address, "Have you not read this scripture?" Second, the image now changes from Jesus as Son to Jesus as Stone.

Parable and Aphorism in Matthew and Luke

The versions in Matt 21:33–43[44] and Luke 20:9–18 will be considered together, as variations on their Markan source. I do not consider that the differences in Luke are enough to warrant postulation of an independent source, closer to *Thomas* than to Mark, which Luke here combines with Mark. I think it more likely Luke judged that Mark's narrative needed some editorial pruning and proceeded accordingly.

Vineyard.   Matt 21:33 is very close to Mark but Luke 20:9 has pruned away almost all allusions to Isa 5:1.

Messengers.   Matt 21:34–36 organizes Mark's messengers into twin sets of plural servants but Luke edits them much more drastically. There are only three single servants and nobody is killed. Once again, this might be evidence of a non-Markan version closer to that of *Thomas*, but it is more likely evidence of Luke's narrative taste.

Murder.   Both Matt 21:37–39 and Luke 20:13–15a have the son killed outside the vineyard, possibly a reference to Jesus' crucifixion outside the city.

Punishment.   In Matt 21:41 this is now a real question and answer dialogue, not just a rhetorical question and answer as in Mark. "When therefore the owner of the vineyard comes, what will he do to those tenants?' They said to him, 'He will put those wretches to a miserable death, and let out the vineyard to other tenants who will give him the fruits in their seasons.'" In Luke 20:15b–16 there is also a dialogue, but a quite different one. "'What then will the owner of the vineyard do to them? He will come and destroy those tenants, and give the vineyard to others.' When they heard this, they said, 'God forbid!'" It is as if everyone gets nervous about this element and how to integrate it into the parable.

Aphorism.   Once again, and even more so, the aphorism is broken from the parabolic closure by "Jesus said to them" in Matt 21:42 and "But he looked at them and said" in Luke 20:16.

Another stone text is appended in Luke 20:18 and it seems that this text was thereafter interpolated into Matt 21:44.

PARABLE AND APHORISM IN TRADITION
Transmission

In this case the transmissional analysis can be summarized in three stages.

First, I presume a parable of Jesus whose plot summary is that given in *Gos. Thom.* 65. This is a perfectly plausible and even historically possible parable of an absentee landlord and his rebellious tenants. It has the standard folkloric threesome (servant, servant, son) and makes certain that we understand why the owner sends his son into a situation which has proved so dangerous, but never lethal, for the servants. He thinks they simply will not accept the authority of the servant. What might such a parable have meant originally for Jesus and his first audience? Negatively, I find it unlikely that the allegorical details extended to Jesus as the Son, so that *Gos. Thom.* 65 was originally a parable of the crucifixion. After the fate of the Baptist, Jesus could very easily have imagined his own violent death but, unless one has proved from other texts that Jesus spoke with some regularity and clarity of himself as Son and heir of God, I find such a reading unlikely, at that early date. I consider that Jesus spoke not about himself but about the Kingdom of God. It was the early church that spoke of him as the Son of God. I also find it unlikely that the original point was warning against the murderous effects of greed. My suspicion is that such a parable probably would need a punishment element to make it securely obvious. And, by the way, if such an element was originally there, I see no reason why *Gos. Thom.* 65 would have removed it since it would have fitted quite well into the overall lesson of *Gos. Thom.* 63–64–65. Nor do I find a reading emphasizing the owner's stupidity particularly convincing after the careful explanation of how the owner misunderstood the situation. Positively, I find most likely a hearing in which the parable, like that of *The Unjust Steward* in Luke 16:1-7 or *The Assassin* in *Gos. Thom.* 98, is a quite shocking example of how evil prepares itself for what it must do while virtue often fails a similar prudence. I thus read it alongside *Gos. Thom.* 98: "The Kingdom of the Father is like a certain man who wanted to kill a powerful man. In his own house he drew his sword and stuck it into the wall in order to find out whether his hand could carry through. Then he slew the powerful man." Both *The Assassin* and *The Evil Tenants* bespeak the smoldering rebellion of urban and rural oppression and are actually possible or even possibly actual examples of how "the sons of this world are more shrewd in dealing with their own generation than the sons of light" (Luke 16:8b). The tenants know how to grasp their chance for the vineyard; do the hearers know how to grasp their chance for the Kingdom of God?

Second, I consider that the separation but juxtaposition of *Gos. Thom.* 65 and 66 cannot be pure coincidence. Beginning from the parabolic summary just outlined, and after the cruci-fixion, the next stage was obvious. Jesus was taken to be the murdered Son of the parable. But that could only be accepted if there was some image for the resurrection within the parable. This was not too easily effected within the narrative plausibility of a realistic parable. But it was done by taking the aphorism about *The Rejected Stone* from Ps 118:22, applying it to Jesus as Stone, and appending it to the parable about Jesus as Son. The sequence and juxtaposition of parable and aphorism gave a full image of crucifixion and resurrection but, of course, there would always be the revealing seam of Jesus as Son and Jesus as Stone. This compound came to *Thomas* so juxtaposed but he either did not see the connection or did not want to use it. At this stage, indeed, the simple juxtaposition was not so compel-lingly obvious that no one could miss it. It may not even have occurred to *Thomas* that the sequence of texts intended to equate the murdered Son and rejected Stone and so to vindicate the Son-as-Stone in a way almost impossible within the narrative constraints of a realisticaly plausible parable.

Third, with one biblical allusion from Ps 118:22 at the end, it was easy to insert another one at the beginning. Indeed, the parable of the vineyard in Isa 5:1–2, the rhetorical questions by God in 5:3–4, the punishment threatened in 5:5–6, and the interpretation of the parable in 5:7, all furnished a model to assist in unifying, as far as possible, parable and aphorism in Mark 12:1–12. The seam between Mark 12:1–8 and 9–11, represented by the change from third to second person, from past to future tense, and from Son to Stone image, could not be erased but the echoes of Isa 5:1–7 might serve to make one forget or ignore it.

Intertextuality

In the first case study involving the parable of *The Great Supper* there was an infiltration from the text of later Christian history, as seen individually and differently by Matthew and Luke, backwards into the earlier parable of Jesus. In the present case, this phenomenon of intertextuality is even more complex. First, of course, there is the interaction of parable and aphorism and the insertion of the latter "within" the former. Second, the text of Christian history has again intertwined itself within the parable and in this case it is seen identically by all three Synoptic writers. There is only the oblique warning of Matthew's own special concerns in his 21:41, "other tenants who will give him the fruits in their seasons," and this is repeated in his own interpretation of the parable in 21:43, "Therefore I tell you, the kingdom of God will be taken away from you and given to a nation producing the fruits of it." Third, however, is a whole new form of intertextuality. Texts from the Old Testament, from Ps 118:22–23 and Isa 5:1–7, have likewise entered the very fabric of the parable. Texts from both past and future, texts which both preceded and succeeded it, have now joined together within the parable uttered between them. Jesus' parable is retold and rephrased, lived and interpreted as a textual matrix of past, present, and future.

This brings up, however, the question of intertextual strain. In the parable of *The Great Supper* some intertextual strain was seen in Luke between the politness and plausibility of the former guests' excuses and the fact that they had been fore-warned of the dinner. Text and event, parable and history strain a little against one another. And the strain was even worse in Matthew where murder and punishment somehow interrupted the wedding feast and where guests dragooned off the streets were expected to be properly attired for the unex-pected feast. This problem of intertextual strain is even more intense in the present instance because we are dealing with both past and future texts intertwined within the text of the parable. Thus, for example, in the Synoptics the owner seems pathetic, stupid, and obtuse. Even after the murder of his ser-vants, and with martial forces at his command, he sends his only son to his death and then finally decides to punish the tenants. Mark and Matthew have this problem, but Luke, as we saw, eliminated it by at least having no murders before the sending of the son. None of this means that intertextuality is invalid, just that it is very difficult to do successfully. We can be grateful for the difficulty of the product since it allows us at this distance still to see the process.

Part Two

EGERTON PAPYRUS 2

The author of the Gospel of John used source materials for the composition of his discourses and dialogues. The *Unknown Gospel* of *Papyrus Egerton 2* further proves that such sources of the Fourth Gospel were directly related to the traditions upon which the Synoptic gospels rest, but also contained "Johannine" elements. These elements are visible in the terminology of the *Unknown Gospel* and in the initial stages of an expansion of sayings into "dialogues" of Jesus.

(Koester, 1980:123)

4 EGERTON PAPYRUS 2 INTRODUCTION

DISCOVERY

Unlike the Oxyrhynchus Papyri which were named for the important early Christian site where they were discovered, the present text is named for the British Museum fund which purchased it. It was discovered "among a collection of papyri purchased last summer [1934] from a dealer" and "the papyri having been purchased (owing to the suspension of the ordinary purchase grant) out of the Bridgewater Fund, it was necessary to include them in the Egerton Collection, and they have therefore been numbered as 'Egerton Papyri'" (Bell & Skeat, 1935a:v).

This section will be concerned with the physical description of what was discovered since so little can be said about where the discovery was actually made. The original editors, Sir H. Idriss Bell, the British Museum's keeper of manuscripts, and T. C. Skeat, his assistant, noted that "unfortunately the provenance of the fragments is unknown. They formed part of a miscellaneous collection bought from a dealer. Most of the papyri acquired with them contain no internal evidence of provenance; of those which do (so far as a preliminary examination goes) one only comes from the Arsinoite nome, five certainly and one probably from Oxyrhynchus; and an Oxyrhynchite origin is likely for the rather high proportion of literary texts. Hence Oxyrhynchus is the most natural place of origin for the Gospel fragments also; but not much weight can really be attached to these arguments" (Bell & Skeat, 1935a: 7). Possibly, then, we are back at Oxyrhynchus.

Oxy P 654 and 655 were written on papyrus scrolls while

Oxy P 1 and the *Gospel of Thomas* were on papyrus codices. Eger P 2 is also from a papyrus codex. The physical description of this text will be of some importance to the interpretation proposed in the case study below so it is necessary to consider papyrus codices in general before looking at Eger P 2 in particular.

Papyrus Codices

There are two separate manufacturing changes reflected in the phrase papyrus codex. One is the implicit change in material from papyrus to parchment. The other is the explicit change in method from scroll to codex.

Papyrus and Parchment. We think of paper as the linen product which came to Europe from China through Baghdad in the eighth century A.D. But almost four thousand years before that time the Egyptians had been making paper from a reed which grew in their shallow and stagnant marshlands. The sticky and triangular pith of this papyrus plant was first cut into long, thin strips. "To make a sheet of papyrus these slices were placed side by side on a hard wooden plank or table with their edges slightly overlapping; on this first layer another was put but with the slices running at right angles to the slices of the first layer. By pressing and beating the two layers became welded together; the tissue thus made was dried under pressure; lastly the surface was polished with some rounded object, possibly of stone, until it became perfectly smooth" (Cěrný: 5–6). The side of the sheet with horizontal fibers is called the recto or front and that with vertical fibers the verso or back.

The first seven Dead Sea Scrolls recovered from Cave 1 at Qumran in 1947 were rolls of leather and this represents a new and rival material to papyrus. Parchment or vellum was prepared from the skins of animals, was sturdier than papyrus, but again had a distinction of sides, now into the hair and flesh side. The transition from papyrus to parchment was taking place about the same time that Christianity apeared.

Scroll and Codex. In ancient Egypt papyrus books were manufactured by pasting about twenty sheets together into a roll, usually with all the recto on one side and the verso on the other. For reasons primarily of fiber stress, the cylinder was rolled with the horizontal fibers inside, and the writing was done in narrow columns primarily but not exclusively on this side. The cylindrical format had existed for three thousand years before the arrival of the newcomer, the codex. This transition was also taking place about the same time that Christianity appeared. "It is in fact becoming increasingly probable that the preference for the codex over the roll was characteristic of the Christian community from quite early in its history, and it may well be that it was to Christianity that the eventual triumph of the former was mainly due" (Bell & Skeat, 1935a:2).

In Latin, a codex was a set of waxed tablets linked together by string along one of their vertical sides and used and reused as a scratch pad. To make a papyrus codex one began with papyrus sheets recto upwards, bent them along a vertical median to produce a quire, and thus each sheet furnished two leaves of four pages. The resultant format was both more economical and more practical and that secured its future. The unbent pile of papyrus had of course a set order of recto-verso. But once it was bent over there was no set order. The sequence now depended on how many sheets in a quire, how many quires in a book, and where, say, two pages fell in the codex. This means that, given only a fragmentary codex page, one would know which was recto and which verso but might not have any idea which followed which, and that could be of some importance as in the case study below.

Four Fragments

Eger P 2 is actually four separate fragments from at least two leaves of a codex. There is a single column of text on recto and verso of the leaves.

Fragment 1. This is about four and a half by three and a

half inches in size and has twenty lines on each side. It is from the centre of the leaf, is damaged along the left margin of the verso and right of the recto, and has other internal damage as well.

Fragment 2.　This is very slightly larger than the first fragment but has only sixteen lines on each side. It is from the top of the leaf, is also damaged along the left margin of the verso and right of the recto, has even more internal damage than the first fragment, and has some indecipherable number, be it for page, leaf, or quire, in top right recto.

Fragment 3.　This is only a scrap of about one by two inches and has very small sections of six lines on each side. It is from the upper corner of a leaf and is also damaged along the left margin of the verso and the right of the recto. This scrap cannot be part of Fragment 2 but could possibly be an upper part of Fragment 1. Bell and Skeat conclude: "The general appearance of the papyrus on the two sides is also not unfavourable to this position; but unfortunately a close examination of the fibres makes it very doubtful. . . . It is always a little unsatisfactory to compare fibres on pieces which are not continuous, and the position suggested for fragment 3 cannot be definitely ruled out, but it is certainly improbable on the evidence of the papyrus, and it seems more likely that this fragment formed part of a third leaf" (1935h:25).

Fragment 4.　This is so small that it contains nothing on the recto and only one doubtful letter on the verso.

DATE

First, when was this manuscript of Eger P 2 written down? In their first and official publication, Bell and Skeat cited paleographic comparisons to date the script in the "middle of the second century" and noted that this date "is highly probable and is likely to err, if at all, on the side of caution, for there are features in the hand which might suggest a period yet earlier in the century" (1935a:1). In their second and more popular publication, that date was still maintained. "The result of a careful examination and comparison of the fragments with other papyri is the conclusion that the manuscript was written not very far from the middle of the second century, with perhaps some preference for a date slightly before over one after A.D. 150. If the upward and downward limits of date be fixed at respectively 130 and 165 we shall probably not be far wrong as to the period within which the manuscript is most likely to have been written" (1935b:10).

Second, and even more important, when was the gospel in Eger P 2 composed? The original editors noted the text's lack of overt doctrinal bias, its matter-of-fact tone, and its use of both "Jesus" and "the Lord" within narrative sections. They concluded that "the total result of these criteria, apart from any detailed consideration of the parallels between the fragments and the canonical Gospels, is to suggest the dates A.D. 80–90 and A.D. 120 as, roughly, the upward and downward limits of the period within which we might expect a Gospel of this character to be composed" (1935b:19).

Bell and Skeat claimed that Eger P 2 "possesses a peculiar importance, for it is unquestionably the earliest specifically Christian manuscript yet discovered in Egypt" (1935a:1). But the same 1934 that produced Eger P 2 produced another major find. This was also a fragment from a papyrus codex. It measured about two and a half by three and a half inches and contained part of John 18:31–33 and 37–38 on either side. Bernard P. Grenfell had obtained it in Egypt as early as 1920 but it had remained unsorted among a pile of papyri in the John Rylands Library at Manchester until 1934 when C. H. Roberts of Oxford University found and published it. He dated it to the first half of the second century. Thus 1934 marked the discovery and 1935 the publication of the two earliest fragments of Christian manuscripts yet discovered. It is extremely interesting that those twin discoveries represent an intracanonical narrative gospel in P 52 (P. Ryl. Gr. 457) and an extracanonical narrative gospel in Eger P 2.

CONTENT

Scenes

There are four scenes on the four mutilated pages represented by the two larger fragments. I shall give them as restored and translated by Bell and Skeat (1935a:28).

Fragment 1 verso contains a *Debate with the Authorities:*

(a) [And Jesus said] unto the lawyers, [?Punish] every wrongdoer doer and transgressor, and not me; . . .
(b) And turning to the rulers of the people he spake this saying, Search the scriptures, in which ye think that ye have life; these are they which bear witness of me.
(c) Think not that I came to accuse you to my Father; there is one that accuseth you, even Moses, on whom you have set your hope.
(d) And when they said, We know well that God spake unto Moses, but as for thee, we know not whence thou art, Jesus answered and said unto them, Now is your unbelief accused . . .

There are extremely close parallels to those last three units in the gospel of John: to (b) at 5:39, to (c) at 5:45, and to (d) at 9:29–30a. Note, however, that in John 9:29–30a the dialogue is not between Jesus and the authorities but between the man born blind and the authorities.

Fragment 1 recto contains what is quite probably the conclusion of the preceding scene and then a whole new scene involving the *Healing of a Leper.* In restored translation the first part reads:

(a) [?they gave counsel to] the multitude to [?carry the] stones together and stone him.
(b) And the rulers sought to lay their hands on him that they might take him and [?hand him over] to the multitude; and they could not take him, because the hour of his betrayal was not yet come.
(c) But he himself, even the Lord, going out through the midst of them, departed from them.

Once again, the closest parallels are in the gospel of John: to (a) at John 8:59a and 10:31, to (b) at 7:30; 7:44; and 10:39a; to (c) at 10:39b. But note, once again, the difference that Eger P 2 refers to the "hour of his betrayal" where John 7:30 refers to "the divinely-ordained 'Hour,' which controls the scheme of the Fourth Gospel from its first introduction in ii.4 to the solemn proclamation in xvii.1" (Dodd: 31).

The second part, the *Healing of a Leper*, reads thus:

> And behold, there cometh unto him a leper and saith, Master Jesus, journeying with lepers and eating with them in the inn I myself also became a leper. If therefore thou wilt, I am made clean. The Lord then said unto him, I will; be thou made clean. And straightway the leprosy departed from him. [And the Lord said unto him], Go [and shew thyself] unto the [priests] . . .

The closest parallel to this is Mark 1:40–44 = Matt 8:1–4 = Luke 5:12–14, but see also Luke 17:14 for the last line.

Fragment 2 recto   contains what the original editors described neutrallly as "The Question of the Tempters" and which I shall argue later is a version of the *Question about Tribute* incident. Their restored translation reads:

> (a) . . . coming unto him began to tempt him with a question, saying, Master Jesus, we know that thou art come from God, for the things which thou doest testify above all the prophets.
> (b) Tell us therefore: Is it lawful [?to render] unto kings that which pertaineth unto their rule? [Shall we render unto them], or not?
> (c) But Jesus, knowing their thought, being moved with indignation, said unto them, Why call ye me with your mouth Master, when ye hear not what I say?
> (d) Well did Isaiah prophesy of you, saying, This people honour me with their lips, but their heart is far from me. In vain do they worship me, [teaching as their doctrines the] precepts [of men] . . .

The closest parallels in this instance represent a mix of Johannine and Synoptic texts from quite disparate locations. These parallels are: to (a), a combination of John 3:2a, "Rabbi, we know that you are a teacher come from God," with a slightly

71

different version of 10:25, "The works that I do in my Father's name, they bear witness to me"; to (b), the doubly stated tribute question at Mark 12:14b-15a = Matt 22:17 = Luke 20:22; to (c), the accusation from the discourse gospel (Q) used by both Matthew and Luke in their versions of Jesus' *Inaugural Sermon*, now at Luke 6:46 and more heavily redacted at Matt 7:21; to (d), the attack on the authorities at Mark 7:6–7 = Matt 15:7–9. It should be underlined that Fragment 2 recto reads smoothly, fluently, and coherently.

Fragment 2 verso   contains a *Miracle by the Jordan*. Bell and Skeat noted that "many suggestions have been made for the restoration of this interesting passage, but none is really satisfactory. . . . A case of miraculous germination (water sprinkled on seed or seed cast on the river) is suggested by what remains, but the indications are not sufficient for any certainty" (1935b: 14). This is their proposed restoration and translation:

> . . . shut up . . . in . . . place . . . its weight unweighed? And when they were perplexed at his strange question, Jesus, as he walked, stood still on the edge of the river Jordan, and stretching forth his right hand he . . . and sprinkled it upon the . . . And then . . . water that had been sprinkled . . . before them and sent forth fruit . . .

There are, of course, no intracanonical parallels to this miracle, however it is to be understood.

Fragment 3 verso   Although one word, "knowing," is certain, "of the text on the verso very little can be restored" (1935b:15).

Fragment 3 recto   The situation here is somewhat better and the fragmentary text seems a parallel to John 10:30–31. Bell and Skeat suggested this restoration:

> [I and my (or the) Father] are one . . . I remain . . . [s]tones to . . . [that they might k]ill [him] . . . saith . . .

As the original editors concluded, "the fragment, small as it is, has value for the Johannine parallel recognized on the recto" (1935b:16).

Sequences

The original editors spent a lot of space insisting that the sequence they gave the four incidents in Eger P 2 was highly conjectural. First, "there is unfortunately no external evidence on this point" (1935a:39), and "there is no external evidence as to the order of the two leaves in the volume" (1935b:10). Second, with regard to internal evidence, the situation is not much better. (1) There is no certainty whether fragment 1 or 2 came first in the codex. (2) There is a good chance that the verso preceded the recto of fragment 1, as we saw in discussing the *Debate with the Authorities* incident. (3) There is no certainty whether the verso or recto of fragment 2 came first: "nor does internal evidence help in determining the order of the two sides of 2, for the text of the recto bears no relation to that of the verso, and it is clear that between the two there was a transition from one episode to another" (1935a:40).

Thus, although Bell and Skeat, and all others thereafter, gave the text in the sequence of 1v, 1r, 2r, 2v as if it was a single quire, they admitted that the order might also have been 2v, 2r, 1v, 1r and that "it would not follow of course that 1 came immediately after 2" (1935a:41). Indeed, in their popular presentation they added that "the appearance of the papyrus, in which the right margin of the verso might well be the outer rather than the inner margin, is perhaps some evidence for the order verso, recto in both fragments" (1935b:11).

The implications of all this rather technical discussion for fragment 2 recto will appear in Case Study 3: *Question about Tribute* below.

INDEPENDENCE

As we have just seen, Eger P 2 has exercised all the possible options for parallels: to Johannine material alone, in the *Debate with the Authorities*, to Synoptic material alone, in the *Healing of a Leper*, to a mixture of Johannine and Synoptic material, in the *Question about Tribute*, and to neither Johannine nor Synoptic material, in the *Miracle at the Jordan*.

Joachim Jeremias, having observed that "the Johannine material is shot through with Synoptic phrases and the Synoptic usage," proposed "the conjecture that the author knew all and every one of the canonical Gospels" but "that the material has been reproduced from memory" (*NTA* 1.95). To which Helmut Koester has rejoined sarcastically that Eger P 2 should then "be treated as a spectacularly early witness for the four-gospel canon" of the New Testament (1980:120).

Synoptic Relations

On the question of synoptic dependence, the first editors vacillated a little. "So far, then, as the Synoptists are concerned, we may conclude that [Eger P 2] appears to represent a quite independent tradition. It is not even certain that its author knew those Gospels at all; if he did, it is in the last degree improbable that he was copying from and embroidering them with the text of one or all of them before him; the most that can be conceded is that he had read them and the words and phrases from them had remained in his memory and found their way into his text" (1935a: 34; see also 1935b:27).

In 1936, however, Dodd argued that the *Healing of a Leper* and *Question about Tribute* incidents in Eger P 2 derived from an oral tradition quite independent of the Synoptics (36, 40). This is also the conclusion of the extremely detailed analysis given in his 1944 Marburg dissertation by the Japanese scholar, Goro Mayeda. Recall, for example, the parallels on fragment 2 recto concerning the *Question about Tribute*. The mention of "Master" in (a) leads smoothly into the "Master" of (c), and the "mouth" in (c) connects smoothly with the "lips" in (d). This is more an integrated composition than a set of randomly remembered phrases from Matthew, Mark, Luke, and John.

Johannine Relations

Here the problem is somewhat more complicated. Bell and Skeat had noted that "some of the verbal parallels with St. John here found are so close that they can hardly be explained except on the supposition of literary contact" and they concluded that "it may perhaps be preferable to conclude either that John and the new Gospel were alike drawing on some earlier source or that the latter was using a form of John earlier than that which we know and widely differing from it" (1935b:28).

In this case Dodd concluded in the opposite direction: "it seems probable that the author of the 'Unknown Gospel' composed one part of his work by abridging and conflating portions of the Fourth Gospel" (32). But here, once again, Mayeda gave detailed arguments against Johannine dependence (see 71–72) and these are extremely persuasive. Note, for example, how smoothly the sequence moves from (b) to (c) to (d) in the *Debate with the Authorities* on fragment 1 verso. Those may be phrases borrowed from different places in John, but they certainly read like a very well integrated composition. Koester even argues that the dependence is in the other direction: "the author of the Fourth Gospel seems to have utilized pieces from the much more tightly composed *Unknown Gospel* in order to construct his elaborate discourses" (1980:123).

I have, therefore, three working hypotheses on Eger P 2. First, it is completely independent of all the intracanonical gospels. Second, considering the random and fragmentary nature of the text and the fact that each leaf gives a curious mix of both Johannine and Synoptic materials, the gospel gives important evidence of a stage in the transmission prior to the separation of those twin traditions. Third, if there is any direct dependence at all, it may well be that both those traditions are dependent on this text, rather than the reverse.

5 CASE STUDY 3
THE QUESTION ABOUT TRIBUTE

The first case study concerned a parable, the second one involved the realationship between a parable and an aphorism. This study discusses a third genre in the Jesus tradition, that of the dialogue. The extant versions of the *Question about Tribute* appear in *Gos. Thom.* 100; in Eger P 2, fragment 2 recto, lines 43–59,and in Mark 12:13–17 = Matt 22:15–22 = Luke 20:20–26.

THE DIALOGUE IN GOS. THOM. 100

In discussing the *Gospel of Thomas* in the first part, I mentioned that certain minimal narrative features are present in *Gos. Thom.* 22, 60, 100. Here is that last text:

> They showed Jesus a gold coin and said to Him, "Caesar's men demand taxes from us." He said to them, "Give Caesar what belongs to Caesar, give God what belongs to God, and give Me what is Mine."

There are two points to be noted in this version of the dialogue.

The first one concerns the coin. The showing of the coin to Jesus has very little point in this account. It is almost like a residue in a gospel which is predominantly discourse.

The second point concerns the word "God" and the final phrase "and give Me what is Mine." If the *Gospel of Thomas* is securely Gnostic, this could be taken as a hierarchical triad, Caesar, God, Jesus; and God would then represent the evil God who created the material world and holds it in bondage. On the one hand, *Thomas* almost never uses the term God. He talks, for example, not of the Kingdom of God but of the Kingdom of My

Father (99), or the Kingdom of Heaven (20, 54, 114), or the Kingdom of the Father (57, 76, 96, 97, 98, 113b), or simply of the Kingdom (3, 22, 46, 49, 82, 107, 109, 113a). On the other hand, it is not clear from his only other usage of God that the term is totally pejorative. This is in *Gos. Thom.* 30, "Where there are three gods, they are gods. Where there are two or one, I am with him." Put mildly, that is not very clear, and we are cast back on the Greek of Oxy P 1, lines 23–27. Harold W. Attridge's recent study of that papyrus under ultraviolet light led him to the following restored translation: "Jesus said, 'Where there are three, they are without god, and where there is but a single one I say that I am with him." He concludes that, "instead of an absolutely cryptic remark about gods being gods, the fragment asserts that any *group* of people lacks divine presence. That presence is available only to the 'solitary one.' The importance of the solitary (*monachos*) is obvious in the Gospel. Cf. Sayings 11, 16, 22, 23, 49, 75 and 106. This saying must now be read in connection with those remarks on the 'monachos.'" (156). But this would also seem to indicate that God is not the evil demiurge of full gnostic dualism. At most God is a term for which *Thomas* usually prefers Father. In *Gos. Thom.* 100, then, it is better not to presume full-flowered gnosticism just on that term alone. *Thomas* did not intend to exalt Jesus above God in a hierarchical triad but simply added a final phrase to an already established dyad of Caesar and God from the tradition. I would presume that his only interest in even mentioning the unit lies in that final addition. Taxes are not his concern, one way or another.

THE DIALOGUE IN EGER P 2

As seen above, the *Question about Tribute* appears on fragment 2 recto, lines 43–59, of this papyrus. There are five literary elements in the narrative: *Test, Compliment, Question, Protest, Accusation.*

Test.   It is clear that there is a trick question involved in this dialogue. The questioners come "to tempt him." The dilemma is, no doubt, that if he answers in the affirmative, he will alienate himself from the nationalists, and if he answers in the negative, he will endanger himself with Herodians and Romans.

Compliment.   In the light of the preceding element, this may be presumed to be less than fully sincere. The address is "Master Jesus," just as in the *Healing of a Leper* on fragment 1 recto, line 33. The address, "Master," that is, Rabbi or Teacher, is quite common for Jesus, and the address "Jesus" is also found if less commonly. But "the address 'Rabbi Jesus' . . . does not correspond with contemporary Jewish usage, and in default of further evidence we must regard it as an imitative form arising in a circle not intimately acquainted with Jewish usages, but aware that Jewish teachers were referred to as Rabbi N. or M.'" (Dodd: 21).

Question.   The question is in double format and is not the specific "taxes to Caesar" of the Synoptics but the more general "unto kings that which pertaineth unto their rule." The Greek word for king, *basileus*, was often used for the Roman Emperor in the eastern provinces so this could easily be a specific reference to Roman imperial taxation even without the name Caesar being used. In Matt 17:25 the question of taxation is discussed and there also the more general title "the kings of the earth" is used.

Protest.   This is Jesus' recognition of their somewhat hypocritical compliment. I already noted the version of this saying in Luke 6:46 and the much more developed one in Matt 7:21(-23). This could be an independent aphorism taken up into these different places. But it must be noted how very precisely it fits into its present context. Its title "Master" refers directly to their preceding and insincere "Master Jesus." And its phrase "with your mouth" is precisely the section omitted in the fragment's succeeding quotation of Isa 29:13. The full text is "Because this people draw near with their mouth and honor me with their lips" but Eger P 2 cites this as, "This people honour me with their lips." I find it very hard to believe that this saying was not originally created as a smooth transition from *Compliment* to *Accusation*. Thereafter, it may have wandered, but I think it wandered from rather than to this present location.

Accusation. The prophetic indictment is introduced with "well did Isaiah prophesy of you," and omits the part just used as a protest from Jesus.

The fragment breaks off at this point and later editors should not conclude with a final period, as do Joachim Jeremias (*NTA* 1.97) and Ron Cameron (75), but with several dots, as did the original editors (Bell & Skeat, 1935a:28; 1935b:13). Indeed, those first editors recognized that "the question is not answered so far as the fragment extends, but it is impossible to say whether or not a reply to it is lost in the lacuna" (1935a:34).

THE DIALOGUE IN THE SYNOPTICS

The version of the *Question about Tribute* appears in Mark 12:13–17 and was thence used by both Matt 22:15–22 and Luke 20:20–26. It has five literary elements: *Test, Compliment, Question, Protest, Answer*. Mark has no equivalent here to the *Accusation* element in Eger P 2, lines 54–59, and this will be considered below in the section on "The Displaced *Accusation* in Mark." But he has the *Answer* element which may have been present in the papyrus but was lost when it was damaged after line 59.

Test. Mark 12:13 does not use the Greek word for "testing" or "tempting" (*peirazein*) which is present in Eger P 2, line 44, at this point in his version, but he does use it in the *Protest* element at 12:15. The words "And they sent to him some of the Pharisees and some of the Herodians, to entrap him in his talk" fulfil the lethal promise of 3:6, "The Pharisees went out, and immediately held counsel with the Herodians against him, how to destroy him."

Compliment. This is a complete rephrasing of the version in Eger P 2, lines 45–47, but it retains the key words, "Master" or "Teacher" and "God." Mark 12:14a is, however, an elegantly construced chiasm:

(a) *"Teacher,* we know that you are
(b) *true,* and care for
(c) *no* man; for you do
(c') *not* regard the position of men, but
(b') *truly*
(a') *teach* the way of God."

The false compliment is an important part of the story and merits literary care.

Question. Mark 12:14b–15a reads "Is it lawful to pay taxes to Caesar, or not? Should we pay them, or should we not?" This retains the double format of the question as in Eger P 2, lines 48–49, but Matt 22:17b and Luke 20:22 both reduce it to a single unit. This is not surprising since a preference for duality is a well-known Markan literary feature (Neirynck, 1982a:24–128).

Protest. Mark 12:15b-16a has *"But* knowing their hypocrisy, *he said to them,* 'Why put *me* to the test?'" On the one hand, this is totally different in content from Eger P 2, lines 50–54 which has, *"But* Jesus, knowing their thought, being moved with indignation, *said unto them, Why* call ye *me* with your mouth Master, when ye hear not what I say." On the other, the format, as indicated by the italicized words in each text, is exactly the same in Greek. And the verbs "test" and "call" are in the second person plural, present tense, in both texts. Mark's protest could easily be a rephrasing of that in the papyrus and, of course, his use of "test" comes from the *Test* element in Eger P 2, line 44.

Answer. Mark 12:15b-18, whose parallel in Eger P 2 is presumably lost in the missing papyrus, will repay careful attention.

1) Construction. The structure is a threefold dialectic of Jesus and Questioners:

EGERTON PAPYRUS 2

    (a) Jesus (12:15b):"'Bring me a coin, and let me look at it.'
        They (12:16a): And they brought one.
    (b) Jesus (12:16b): And he said to them, 'Whose likeness and
        inscription is this?'
        They (12:16c): They said to him, 'Caesar's.'
    (c) Jesus (12:17): Jesus said to them, 'Render to Caesar the things
        that are Caesar's, and to God the things that are God's.'
        They (12:18): And they were amazed at him."

This triple interchange is maintained in Matt 22:19–22, reduced to a double one in Luke 20:24–26, and, as we saw earlier, appears as only a single interchange in *Gos. Thom.* 100.

2) Coin. Notice how Mark 12:15b-16a slows down the entire narrative: *"'Bring* me' ... And they *brought."* The narrative remains, as it were, in suspension while the questioners go to get the coin. They do not have it with them in Mark but must leave the scene to get it. The temporal wait between "bring me" and "they brought" underlines for the reader the importance of the coin in the story's plot. This is somewhat reduced by Matt 22:19, *"Show* me' ... And they *brought,"* and is totally absent from Luke 20:24 with his, *"Show* me a coin," and thereafter he goes immediately into Jesus' question about the likeness. And, needless to say, the whole importance of the coin is lost in *Gos. Thom.* 100 where the questioners themselves bring it to Jesus. Why the coin is so significant will apear in the next section on Caesar.

3) Caesar. From its start this narrative has a double focus, that of question and answer, entrapment and escape. They intend to combine question and entrapment but Jesus counters by combining answer and escape. They plan "to entrap him in his talk," according to Mark 12:13, but instead Jesus succeeds in entrapping them in their own words. Prompted by him, they themselves bring the coin, and again prompted by him, they themselves have to admit whose image it contains. This counter-entrapment is even more obvious in Mark's Greek than in that of either Matthew or Luke, and it is also more

obvious in the original language than in English translation. Mark 12:17 has cited Jesus' word "Caesar's" as early in the pronouncement as possible, even prior to the verb "render" itself. The effect might be shown in English like this: "They said to him, 'Caesar's.' Jesus said to them, 'Caesar's render to Caesar and God's to God.'" The Greek of Matt 22:21 and Luke 20:25 reverses the order to the more usual sequence (literally): "'Render Caesar's to Caesar and God's to God.'" Segments of the Markan textual tradition later effected this same change on Mark himself. This submission of specific rhetoric to general grammar can thus be traced over three stages: (1) Mark in Greek: Caesar's/render/to Caesar; (2) Matthew and Luke in Greek: Render/Caesar's/Caesar; (3) Synoptics in English: Render/ to Caesar/Caesar's. So much, then, for Mark's attempt to underline how Jesus counter-trapped them in their own words by keeping their "Caesar's" and his "Caesar's" as syntactically close as possible. But, in any case, the narrative's power concerns how they set out to entrap Jesus in his speech and were entrapped instead in their own.

THE DISPLACED ACCUSATION IN MARK

I presume a more original version of the *Question about Tribute* composed of six elements: *Test, Compliment, Question, Protest, Accusation, Answer*. Of those six, the first five were present in Eger P 2, lines 43–59, since the final one was lost in the papyrus' mutilation. And of those six, only five are in Mark 12:13–17, since this lacks the *Accusation* from Isa 29:13. I propose that Mark himself relocated this unit to 7:6–7 as part of the composition of 7:1–23.

The Accusation in Mark 7

The use of Isa 29:13 in Eger P 2 refers it to Jesus himself and the emphasis is on the first part of the verse. That in Mark 7 refers it to God and emphasizes rather the second part of the verse.

83

In 7:3, 4, 5 the Pharisaic teachings are called "the tradition of the elders . . . traditions . . . the traditions of the elders." Then in 7:6–7 there is the accusation from the Greek Septuagint translation of Isa 29:13, "Well did Isaiah prophesy of you hypocrites, as it is written, 'This people honors me with their lips, but their heart is far from me; in vain do they worship me, teaching as doctrines the precepts *of men.*'" Finally, in 7:8, 9, 13 there is another threefold mention of "the tradition *of men* . . . your tradition . . . your tradition." The italicized words note how Mark fits the text into its context.

It may be noted in passing that Col 2:22 also alludes to the latter part of Isa 29:13 in a similar context: "Why do you submit to regulations, 'Do not handle, Do not taste, Do not touch' (referring to things which all perish as they are used), according to human precepts and doctrines."

Two arguments convince me that the citation of Isa 29:13 is Mark's relocation of the *Accusation* element from Eger P 2, lines 54–59. First, there is the introduction: *"well did* Isaiah prophesy of you." This formulation appears only here in Mark 7:6 = Matt 15:7 and in Acts 28:25. Matthew is obviously dependent for the expression on Mark but so also is Acts. Barnabas Lindars has observed that "the similarity between Acts 28.25b and Mark 7.6a is thus not accidental. Luke omitted a large slice of Mark (6.45–8.26) . . . dominated by the hardened blindness both of the scribes and Pharisees and of the disciples themselves . . . Luke saves this up for the end of Acts. Here we find Paul giving a similar indictment against the Jews" (166). I consider, therefore, that this unusual introduction, "well did . . . " came from Eger P 2, line 54, into Mark 7:6, and thence into both Matt 15:7 and Acts 28:25. Second, the phrase "This people honors me with their lips" is incomplete. It should read "This people draw near *with their mouth* and honor me with their lips." We have already seen that Eger P 2 omitted "draw near *with their mouth*" in order to have Jesus protest "Why call ye me *with your mouth* Master." There is, however, no very obvious reason why Mark would have omitted part of the first phrase, except that he was taking it over unchanged from that location in Eger P 2.

THE DIALOGUE IN TRADITION

Transmission

There are two types of dialogues in the Jesus tradition, and their modes and laws of transmission may be quite distinct.

One type could be termed an *aphoristic dialogue* because it takes an independent dialogue and locates it interpretatively within a question and answer format. In this type of dialogue the saying of Jesus is prior to its setting. A very appropriate example occurs in that chapter of Mark just discussed. In Mark 7:14 Jesus "called the people to him" and in 7:15 he offers them this saying: "There is nothing outside a man which by going into him can defile him; but the things which come out of a man are what defile him." Next, in 7:17, "when he had entered the house, and left the people, his disciples asked him about the parable." In order to answer them, Jesus splits the aphorism of 7:15 into its twin halves. He first repeats 7:15a in 7:18 and then explains it in 7:19; he next repeats 17:15b in 7:20 and then explains it in 7:21–23. This is a classic case of aphoristic dialogue. Mark composed the entire dialogue of 7:17–23 around the traditional aphorism in 7:15.

A second type could be called an *integrated dialogue* because here the question, comment, or request, and the answer, response, or reply, were always a unified whole. In this type of dialogue the saying of Jesus was simultaneous with its setting from the very beginning of the tradition.

I propose that the *Question about Tribute* is not an aphoristic dialogue, that is, a setting built up around the originally independent saying, "Render to Caesar the things that are Caesar's, and to God the things that are God." I do not think that Jesus saw the world as so divided between twin powers. I think that this was always an integrated dialogue, was always something of a trick answer to a trick question. It forced the questioners to admit that the coinage bore Caesar's image and should therefore be returned to him. It did not, however, really answer the general but in this case insincere question about taxes.

In this case the transmission can be reconstructed over three stages. A first stage is in Eger P 2, fragment 2 recto, lines 43–59, but is broken off at line 59 so that the *Answer* to the question is no longer present. A second stage is in Mark 12: 13–17 which is directly dependent on the papyrus text. It might be possible that Mark is dependent on some other version exactly similar to Eger P 2 but I prefer not to multiply entities just out of nervousness. Mark's major change over his source was to relocate the *Accusation* element to his new composition in 7:6–7, but there it still trails telltale indications of its origin. A third stage is in *Gos. Thom.* 100 and this is a good warning not to presume that the shortest text is always the earliest. The tradition can abbreviate as well as lengthen a unit in transmission. *Thomas* added on "and to Me what is Mine," which is probably the only way he can see to make the saying of interest. The dialogic format is still present but barely so. The coin is brought by the questioners and serves no useful purpose in the narrative.

One watches the dialogue steadily shorten from Eger P 2, to Mark, to Luke, to *Thomas*, and sees a dialogue slowly tending to become an aphorism. Finally, one begins to cite the saying of Jesus all by itself, as if it divided the world into twin powers, God and Caesar. But the meaning of the saying depends absolutely on its setting, on the fact that it was uttered in dialectic, as a trick answer to a trick question.

Intertextuality

In the first part I mentioned how texts such as Ps 118:22–23 and Isa 5:1-7 had entered the very fabric and interpretation of the parable of *The Evil Tenants*. In the present case Isa 29:13 appears first as part of the *Question about Tribute* in Eger P 2, fragment 2r, lines 54–59. Here it refers the biblical text to Jesus himself and casts the emphasis on the first part of the verse. Thereafter, it is transferred by Mark from his version of that incident to a new location at 7:6–7. There it refers, as it did originally, to God and the emphasis is now on the second part of the verse. Intertextuality, then, has a certain wandering quality. Once the Old Testament text has entered the Jesus tradition at one or another place, it can easily be transferred to others thereafter.

Part Three

THE SECRET GOSPEL OF MARK

To them, therefore, as I said above, one must never give way; nor, when they put forward their falsifications, should one concede that the secret Gospel is by Mark, but should even deny it on oath. For, "Not all true things are to be said to all men."

From the letters of the most holy Clement

6 THE SECRET GOSPEL OF MARK INTRODUCTION

DISCOVERY

Nothing is simple about this text and it has even been suggested that complexity masks duplicity. My opening quotation from the document intends to underline that aura of suspicion which hangs over the entire discussion.

In baldest summary: (1) Morton Smith has reported his discovery (2) of an incomplete copy (3) of a letter from Clement of Alexandria (4) concerning the Carpocratians and (5) discussing different versions of Mark's gospel. Those five items may serve as headings.

Reported Discovery

The Greek orthodox monastery of Mar Saba is located in the Judean wilderness about half way between Bethlehem and the Dead Sea. In the winter of 1941, Morton Smith, then a Harvard Divinity School graduate student marooned by war on the wrong side of the Atlantic, visited the monastery for the first time.

> I had often heard of Mar Saba. With St. Catherine's, it was one of the two great desert monasteries of the Orthodox Church, monasteries in which the Byzantine order of services and way of life were still preserved. St. Saba—in Arabic, Mar Saba—its founder, had lived in the fifth century, roughly a thousand five hundred years ago, and ever since, with brief interruptions, there had been some sort of monastic life at the site. . . . In their free moments the monks showed me around the monastery and also took me to visit some of the caves that lined the walls of the wadi on both sides up and down stream. Many of the caves had formerly been the homes of hermits, and in

some one could still see the remains of old paintings and inscriptions. In a few of them, I was told, fragments of manuscripts had been found. . . . I was shown the two libraries, as I was the other sights of the monastery, but at the time I paid them little attention. My main interest was in the services, which gave me a new understanding of worship as a means of disorientation (1973a:2, 4, 5).

In the summer of 1958 he returned for a second visit to Mar Saba but now as Professor Morton Smith of Columbia University, with permission to spend a few weeks in the monastery library locating and cataloguing its manuscripts. This was not quite as obvious a process as it might appear.

At present, copying is generally done on ordinary paper. But formerly paper was rare and expensive, so every spare page of available books was pressed into use. . . . Not only end papers and blank pages, but even margins often contain considerable manuscript additions. Another thing to be noticed is the binding. Because paper was rare and expensive, old manuscripts were used to bind new books. For instance, one printed book in Mar Saba has not only received important manuscript additions fore and aft, but has, for end pages, pages from a late mediaeval Georgian manuscript of the life of St. Onophrius . . . Beneath the Georgian end papers . . . were cardboards made of layers on layers of old manuscripts glued together. On top was a twelfth-century Greek liturgical text, below that came another Georgian manuscript, then an eleventh-century Greek liturgical text, then an Arabic text, almost effaced, then one even more obscure, perhaps in Hebrew, then another Georgian text, and finally a tenth-century Greek liturgical text. . . . We know from [such] bindings . . . (and there are many like them) that fragments of old manuscripts were easily available down to the middle of the last century (1960:173, 174, 176; note photographs).

This rather accidental, somewhat casual, and decidedly functional conservation of old manuscripts was the background for Smith's most startling discovery: "The manuscripts of Mar Saba proved, on examination, to be mostly modern. This was no surprise, since it was well known that the rich collection of ancient manuscripts, for which the monastery was famous in the early nineteenth century, had been transferred to Jerusalem for safekeeping in the eighteen-sixties. . . . Among the items examined was one, number 65 in my published notes, of which the manuscript element consisted of two and a half pages of writing at the back of an old printed book" (Smith, 1973b:ix).

My concern will be with those two and a half pages: 1 recto with 28 lines, 1 verso with 26 lines, and 2 recto with 18 lines (Smith, 1973:448–453). I shall refer to the whole document as the *Mar Saba Letter of Clement* in order to distinguish that whole from the part concerning the *Secret Gospel of Mark*. I shall be referring, therefore, to *MSLC* 1r:1–28, 1v:1–26, 2r:1–18.

Incomplete Copy

The text was copied at the back of

> an exemplar of Isaac Voss's edition of the *Epistulae genuinae S. Ignatii Martyris* (Amsterdam: J.Blaeu, 1646). . . . The manuscript was written over both sides of the last page (which was blank) of the original book and over half the recto of a sheet of binder's paper. The binding was of that heavy, white paperboard so often found on books bound in Venice during the seventeenth and eighteenth centuries. Therefore the date of the book, plus about fifteen or twenty years (1660 or 1665), may be taken as the date *after* which the manuscript insertion was probably made . . . As for the date at which it was probably made, that can be settled only by dating the hand . . . The consensus . . . would date the hand about 1750, plus or minus about fifty years (Smith, 1973b:1).

The document begins "From the letters of the most holy Clement, the author of the Stromateis. To Theodore" (1r:1). It concludes in the middle of a sentence, "Now the true explanation and that which accords with the true philosophy . . ." (2r:18). But why would somebody around 1750 have made an incomplete copy of a letter of Clement of Alexandria in the back of a collection of the letters of Ignatius of Antioch? Here is what can be considered at best a possible scenario.

First, there is evidence that a collection of the letters of Clement of Alexandria existed at Mar Saba at least in the period 715–50 when John of Damascus cited from them (Smith,

1973b:6, 285, 288). Second, since there is no record of this collection from elsewhere, it may have remained there undisturbed until it was destroyed in a disastrous fire, dated in the early eighteenth century by J. Phokylides, the monastery's historian. "The fire burned out the contents of a cave in which many of the antiquities and the oldest MSS of the monastery had been stored. Since the fire was in a cave the air supply must have been limited. Present monastic tradition says the fire smouldered for two weeks before the monks could get through the smoke to put it out. Even under the most favorable conditions books are difficult to burn; they usually char around the edges and then go out. Therefore it is presumable that after the fire a large number of loose leafs, almost undamaged, were salvaged from the unburned centers of old MSS" (Smith, 1973b: 289). Third, and this must be underlined as no more than hypothesis, "the fragmentary state of the present letter is best explained by supposing it a copy of such an isolated leaf. . . . No doubt someone's attention was attracted by the surprising content of this isolated folio. He studied the text, corrected it to the best of his ability, and then copied it into the back of the monastery's edition of the letters of Ignatius, since it resembled them in being a letter from an early father, attacking gnostic heretics" (Smith, 1973b:289).

Clementine Letter

The letter was from Clement of Alexandria, who was born Titus Flavius Clemens, possibly at Athens, of pagan parents around 150 A.D. After his conversion to Christianity he travelled extensively in southern Italy, Syria, and Palestine. He finally settled at Alexandria where he succeeded Pantaenus as head of the catechetical school around the year 200. A few years later he fled Egypt during the persecution under Septimius Severus (193–211) and settled in Cappadocia with his pupil Alexander, later bishop of Jerusalem. Clement never returned to Alexandria but died in exile shortly before 215 (Quasten: 2.5).

94

His major extant writings are the *Protrepticus* or *Exhortation to the Greeks*, the *Paedagogus* or *Instructor*, and the *Stromateis* or *Miscellanies*. It is as "author of the Stromateis" (1r:1) that he is identified by the letter's copier. There is also a shorter work, *Quis Dives Salvetur?* or *The Rich Man's Salvation*, which intends to reassure rich Christians that it is the use and not the fact of wealth that counts before God.

The letter was to one, Theodore, who is otherwise unknown. "The name was common in Jewish and thence in Christian circles and could easily have been that of a correspondent in Palestine" (Smith, 1973b:7).

Is the letter really from Clement or is it one of the pseudepigraphical epistles so common in those early Christian centuries? Smith presented detailed linguistic, stylistic, and material comparisons with the works of Clement in his original publication (1973b:6–85). He has summed up the situation more recently by saying that "most scholars would attribute the letter to Clement, though a substantial minority are still in doubt. . . . Meanwhile, the recent 'provisional' inclusion of the letter in the Berlin edition of Clement's works adequately indicates its actual status" (1982:451–52).

Carpocratian Gnostics

Clement opens the letter with a commendation for Theodore: "You did well in silencing the unspeakable teachings of the Carpocratians. For these are the 'wandering stars' referred to in the prophecy, who wander from the narrow road of the commandments into a boundless abyss of the carnal and bodily sins" (1r:2–4). Who are these unspeakable Carpocratians against whom Clement invokes the words of Jude 13?

Kurt Rudolph summed up Gnostic ethics by observing how "the rejection of the creation and the simultaneous appeal to the possession of celestial knowledge led to a rejection of the conventional conceptions of morality. Two contrary and extreme conclusions could be drawn: the libertine or amoralistic and the

ascetic. Both expressed the same basic attitude: a protest against
the pretensions of the world and its legislative ruler; a revolu-
tion on a moralistic plane" (253). George MacRae, in discussing
why the early church eventually rejected gnosticism, cites in
first place this problem of non-conformist ethical behavior. He
finds a very early example of this in 1 Cor 5:3–5: "The inces-
tuous man is best understood as one who flouts the morality
that is customary 'even among pagans' on religious grounds
based on a Gnostic or quasi-Gnostic scorn for material existence. .... The traditionally alleged Gnostic libertine stance is
perfectly illustrated not only in his behavior, but in the community's proud tolerance of it—which is more properly the object
of Paul's indignation" (1980:128).

Among those Gnostic sects who advocated such programmatic and even cultic antinomianism the Carpocratians are
given greatest attention by both Irenaeus of Lyons and Clement
of Alexandria, contemporaries writing in the last quarter of the
second century.

Irenaeus' volume *Against Heresies* devotes a chapter to the
Carpocratians. "They lead a licentious life, and to conceal their
impious doctrines, they abuse the name [of Christ], as a means
of hiding their wickedness; so that 'their condemnation is just'
[Rom 3:8], when they receive from God a recompense suited to
their works. So unbridled is their madness, that they declare
they have in their power all things which are irreligious and
impious, and are at liberty to practice them; for they maintain
that things are evil or good, simply in virtue of human opinion."
But this libertinism has a theoretical justification and a programmatic character. "They deem it necessary, therefore, that
by means of transmigration from body to body, souls should
have experience of every kind of life as well as every kind of
action (unless, indeed, by a single incarnation, one may be able
to prevent any need for others, by once for all, and with equal
completeness, doing all those things which we dare not either
speak or hear of, nay, which we must not even conceive in our

INTRODUCTION

thoughts, nor think credible, if any such thing is mooted among those persons who are our fellow-citizens), in order that, as their writings express it, their souls, having made trial of every kind of life, may, at their departure, not be wanting in any particular" (1.25.3–4; *ANF:* 1.94–95). Notice especially the phrase I have italicized in this final quotation: "And in their writings we read as follows, the interpretation which they give [of their views], declaring that *Jesus spoke in a mystery to his disciples and apostles privately*" (1.25.5; *ANF:* 1.96).

Clement's *Miscellanies* proposes a fundamental distinction between libertine and ascetic Gnostics, and even subsumes the latter under the former. "We may divide all the heresies into two groups in making answer to them. Either they teach that one ought to live on the principle that it is a matter of indifference whether one does right or wrong, or they set a too ascetic tone and proclaim the necessity of continence on the ground of opinions which are godless and arise from hatred of what God has created. First we may discuss the former group. If it is lawful to live any sort of life one likes, obviously one may live in continence; or if any kind of life has no dangers for the elect, obviously one of virtue and self-control is far less dangerous" (3.5.40; Oulton & Chadwick:58). When he speaks, sarcastically, of "the doctrines of the excellent Carpocratians," he writes that "these, so they say, and certain other enthusiasts for the same wickedness, gather together for feasts (I would not call their meeting an Agape), men and women together. After they have sated their appetites ('on repletion Cypris, the goddess of love, enters' as it is said [by Euripides]), then they overturn the lamps and so extinguish the light that the shame of their adulterous 'righteousness' is hidden, and they have intercourse where they will and with whom they will" (3.2.10; Oulton & Chadwick: 45). Clement concludes the chapter by suggesting, "Of these and other similar sects Jude, I think, spoke prophetically in his letter—'In the same way also these dreamers' (for they do not seek to find the truth in the light of day) as

97

far as the words 'and their mouth speaks arrogant things'" (3.2.11; Oulton & Chadwick: 45). This refers to Jude 8–16 and one recalls the reference to Jude 13 cited against the Carpocratians in the Mar Saba letter (1r:3).

Even if we recognize that immorality is a standard accusation in religious polemic, and even if much Gnostic antinomianism was theory rather than practice, it is this Carpocratian libertinism which stands as the background of the Clementine letter.

Versions of Mark

This is, of course, the heart of the matter. After commending Theodore for his opposition to the Carpocratians (1r:2–11), Clement starts to answer his questions concerning their version of Mark's gospel: "Now of the things they keep saying about the divinely inspired Gospel according to Mark, some are altogether falsifications, and others, even if they do contain some true elements, nevertheless are not reported truly. For the true things being mixed with inventions, are falsified, so that, as the saying goes, even the salt loses its savor" (1r:11–15).

Clement makes two sets of distinctions. First, there is the distinction between oral and written tradition. Mark did not and should not have written down the most esoteric secrets of the oral tradition: "Nevertheless, he yet did not divulge the things not to be uttered, nor did he write down the hierophantic teaching of the Lord" (1r:22–24). Smith, following Maurice Wiles, suggests that "Clement's mention of them was intended to assure Theodore that although the Carpocratians had got hold of the secret Gospel they had not learned the highest secrets" (1973b:35). Second, there are actually three different versions of Mark's written gospel under discussion. I shall not complicate this any further than necessary by suggesting a fourth version, "Canonical Mark." As far as can be seen from Clement's quotations of Public Mark, this is synonymous with our present canonical Mark.

The Public Gospel of Mark. Clement describes this as follows. "As for Mark, then, during Peter's stay in Rome he wrote an account of the Lord's doings, not, however declaring all of them, nor yet hinting at the secret ones, but selecting what he thought most useful for increasing the faith of those who were being instructed" (1r:15–18). This gospel would be available to those taking instruction before baptism and so would be relatively public.

The Secret Gospel of Mark. "But when Peter died a martyr, Mark came over to Alexandria, bringing both his own notes and those of Peter, from which he transferred to his former book the things suitable to whatever makes for progress toward knowledge. Thus he composed a more spiritual Gospel for the use of those who were being perfected . . . to the stories already written he added yet others and, moreover, brought in certain sayings of which he knew the interpretation would, as a mystagogue, lead the hearers into the innermost sanctuary of the truth hidden by seven veils. Thus, in sum, he prepared matters, neither grudgingly nor incautiously, in my opinion, and, dying, he left his composition to the church in Alexandria, where it even yet is most carefully guarded, being read only to those who are being initiated into the great mysteries" (1r:18–1v:2). Accordingly, *Secret Mark* is not a separate gospel but an amplified version of *Public Mark*. Furthermore, the amplification was from the original store of written Petrine tradition. Smith thinks that "those who are being perfected" may refer "*either* to baptism *or* to some initiatory ceremony other than baptism *or* to a long process of perfection in gnosis" (1973b:34).

The Carpocratian Gospel of Mark. "But since the foul demons are always devising destruction for the race of men, Carpocrates, instructed by them and using deceitful arts, so enslaved a certain presbyter of the church in Alexandria that he got from him a copy of the secret Gospel, which he both interpreted according to his blasphemous and carnal doctrine and, moreover, polluted, mixing with the spotless and holy words utterly shameless lies. From this mixture is drawn off the teaching of the Carpocratians" (1v:2–10). For Clement, then, *Carpocratian Mark* is an amplified version of *Secret Mark*. He proposes, in other words, a simple stemma: from *Public* to *Secret* to *Carpocratian* versions of Mark.

It is interesting that Clement has to admit the Carpocratians have a copy of *Secret Mark*. He never suggests that they do not have it, or that such a text does not exist. In fact, his best or worst suggestion is this: "To them, therefore, as I said above, one must never give way; nor, when they put forward their falsifications, should one concede that the secret Gospel is by Mark, but should deny it on oath" (1v:10–12).

The major question, then, to be discussed later, is how does the content of these three versions as cited by Clement (1v:20–2r:16) relate to the canonical gospel of Mark. But first there is an even more important question.

FORGERY?

In this section of the introduction I usually turn to questions of provenance or date. But in this one case there is the possibility of modern forgery and that puts provenance and date in a rather different light.

The authenticity of a text can only be established by the consensus of experts who have studied the original document under scientifically appropriate circumstances. Twenty-five years after the original discovery this has not yet happened and that casts a cloud over the entire proceedings. One can, according to taste, blame all sorts of individuals and institutions for this failure. One can fault Morton Smith, fairly or unfairly, for not obtaining immediate expert confirmation and collaboration *in situ* at Mar Saba. One might also fault him for not swiftly publishing a facsimile edition with full physical and factual data but minimal personal and interpretative proposals. One could also wonder if Harvard University Press made any attempt to obtain independent verification and new professional photographs in preparing Morton Smith's manuscript for publication fifteen years after the discovery. Finally, a decade after Smith's scholarly and popular books made the discovery fully public, one wonders why more scholars have not visited Mar Saba to report on the situation.

The only published report concerning the present status of the text that I know of is this one from Thomas J. Talley. "My own attempts to see the manuscript in January of 1980 were frustrated, but as witnesses to its existence I can cite the Archimandrite Meliton of the Jerusalem Greek Patriarchate who, after the publication of Smith's work, found the volume at Mar Saba and removed it to the patriarchal library, and the patriarchal librarian, Father Kallistos, who told me that the manuscript (two folios) has been removed from the printed volume and is being repaired. Such, at least, was the state of affairs in 1980" (45).

The essential problem, then, is the lack of several independent studies of the *original* document by experts on Greek handwriting. Private responses to necessarily amateur photographs were quite good enough to start the process of verification but are utterly inadequate to conclude it. There are bound to be doubts about authenticity when the experts have only seen "photographs of the manuscript" (Smith, 1973b:1).

There is, however, another difficulty which has, rightly or wrongly, compounded that first and more important one. Smith's scholarly presentation of his discovery included three major sections. One involved "The Letter" section of the manuscript and argued quite convincingly for its Clementine authenticity (1973b: 5–85). Another involved "The Secret Gospel" and proposed, again quite convincingly, certain possible relationships between *Secret Mark* and the intracanonical gospels (1973b:87–194). But there was also a section on "The Background" (1973b:195–278). The basic thesis of this chapter is that the Carpocratians got it right, that *Carpocratian Mark*, and not

Public Mark or *Secret Mark*, was the faithful heir of the authentic
Jesus tradition. Smith proposed there "a definition of 'the
mystery of the kingdom of God': It was a baptism administered
by Jesus to chosen disciples, singly, and by night. In this baptism the disciple was united with Jesus. The union may have
been physical . . . there is no telling how far symbolism went in
Jesus' rite . . . but the essential thing was that the disciple was
possessed by Jesus' spirit. One with Jesus, he participated in
Jesus' ascent into the heavens; he entered the kingdom of God
and was thereby set free from the laws ordained for and in the
lower world" (1973b:251). I found this chapter as unconvincing
as the previous two were convincing. It is not of course an
impossible interpretation of the powerfully generative hermeneutical ambiguities inaugurally present in the parables and
miracles of Jesus. It is precisely the type of interpretation proposed by libertine gnosticism and one need only read Irenaeus
or Clement to see how the Carpocratians, for example, could
derive their theory and practice from the words and deeds of
the Jesus tradition.

When one brings together a document neither verified nor
available in its *original* rescription and a theory about Jesus as a
possibly homosexual baptizer, the mixture is volatile enough
for accusation and sensation. Quentin Quesnell has noted that
a convincingly detailed forgery of Clement's style could not
have been done before this century. "In 1936 Stählin published
Volume IV of his critical edition of the works of Clement. 828
pages of that volume are devoted to final summary indexing.
Clement's vocabulary is covered on pp. 197–828. Every occurrence listed is accompanied with a quotation long enough to
show how the word is used in context. Words of more frequent
occurrence are conveniently subdivided" (1975:55). This means
that, if the Mar Saba letter is a forgery, it must have been forged
after 1936. Smith replied: "Quesnell insinuates that I forged the
MS" (1976:197). Quesnell responded: "If that had been my
point, I would have stated it clearly" (1976:200). But later Smith

still maintained that "Quesnell's denial was part of an absurd attempt to prove me the author of the text. Unfortunately, nobody else has so high an opinion of my classical scholarship" (1982:450). If the text is a forgery, then, one might presume that the scholarship used by Smith to authenticate the document in 1973 was actually prepared to forge it in 1958.

My own position is that independent study of the *original* manuscript is absolutely necessary for scholarly certitude; that this should be kept carefully apart from judgments on Clementine ethics or Carpocratian practices; and that all of that should be kept separate from whether one likes or dislikes Morton Smith's personality, methods, or proposals. In the meanwhile, however, and pending fuller external study of the manuscript, my own procedure is to accept the document's authenticity as a working hypothesis and to proceed with internal study of its contents.

CONTENT

I am now exclusively concerned with the content of *Secret Mark* as described by Clement (*MSLC* 1v:19–2r:18).

Theodore wants to know whether certain items in *Carpocratian Mark* really appear in *Secret Mark*. Clement tells Theodore, "To you, therefore, I shall not hesitate to answer the questions you have asked, refuting the falsifications by the very words of the Gospel" (1v:19–20). Clement is thus citing from *Secret Mark*.

He makes two points. First, positively, he tells him what is present in *Secret Mark* and I outline it as in Figure 1.

Second, negatively, he tells him what is not in *Secret Mark* but presumably was claimed in *Carpocratian Mark*. There are two statements. After citing *SGM* 1–3 he says "but 'naked man with naked man,' and the other things about which you wrote, are not found" (2r:13–14). And after citing *SGM* 4–5 he adds "but the many other things about which you wrote both seem to be and are falsifications" (2r:17).

Figure 1

MSLC	SGM	Canonical Mark	Subject
(1) 1v:21–22	SGM 1	=Mark 10:32–34	*Third Passion Prophecy*
(2) 1v:23–2r:11	SGM 2		*The Resurrected Youth*
(3) 2r:11–13	SGM 3	=Mark 10:35(–45?)	*James and John*
(4) 2r:14	SGM 4	=Mark 10:46a	*Arrival at Jericho*
(5) 2r:14–16	SGM 5		*Jesus and theWomen*

Basically, then, we are talking about two units not found in our canonical Mark, *SGM* 2 after 10:32–34 and *SGM* 5 after 10:46a.

INDEPENDENCE

Although Johannine and Markan features are interwoven throughout *Secret Mark* I shall separate them here for the convenience of my own presentation. I presume throughout, of course, the far more complete and detailed analysis of Smith (1973b:87–194).

Johannine Relations

In the tabular outline given above there was no parallel for *SGM* 2 (1v:23–2r:11) in canonical Mark but there is, of course, an obvious parallel in the raising of Lazarus in John 11. What is the most likely relationship between these two texts?

Smith, having detailed the specifically redactional traits in John 11, asserted that "there can be no question that the story in the longer text of Mk. is more primitive in form than the story of Lazarus in Jn. Further, it is impossible to suppose that the author of the longer text of Mk. used, or even knew, the Johannine Lazarus story. Had he known it, his text would certainly have shown at least some of the secondary Johannine traits listed above. Since it has none of them, it must be completely independent of Jn." (1973b:156). Brown countered by saying that "in my opinion Smith's thesis about the relationship of SGM to John is more reasonable than his theses about the relationship of SGM to the Synoptic Gospels. Nevertheless, I would still judge that *it is not impossible* that SGM drew upon John. True, I do not think that the evidence *clearly* points to the opposite conclusion, namely, dependence of SGM upon John; but I do think that a case can be made for dependence" (470, 474). When Smith used "impossible" it was easy for Brown to claim "it is not impossible." But the more realistic question concerns a delicate balance of plausibility. It is certainly possible to suggest reasons why SGM 2 might have read John 11 and removed absolutely everything that was characteristically Johannine. But is this more plausible than the alternative possibility, namely, that SGM 2 represents a more primitive version of the miracle story?

There are three small and rather delicate points which tip the balance for me towards Smith's position of independence from John 11.

Voice. In SGM 2 "a great cry was heard from the tomb" (2r:1) but in John 11:43 it is Jesus who "cried with a loud voice" (literally, "a great cry"). I find the more plausible change here to be from SGM 2 to John rather than the reverse. In Mark, for example, a "great cry" is uttered both by demons as Jesus exorcizes them (1:26; 5:7) and by Jesus himself as he dies (15:34, 37). In SGM 2, then, it has overtones of the struggle with the demonic power of death. But John never uses it elsewhere, and in 11:43 it seems at best a residue.

Anger. After the prostrate request of the dead man's sister and before Jesus proceeds to the tomb, SGM 2 talks of him "being angered" (1v:25) and so also does John 11:33,38. In this latter case, however, the verb is different and is translated as "deeply moved." However, the term's usage elsewhere in the New Testament indicates negative emotion, such as anger, in Matt 9:30 and Mark 1:43; 14:5. That was also the meaning we saw for it in Eger P 2, 2r:51. There seems no reason for anger in

John and hence the more general translation. Once again, I find the change to be more likely from *SGM* 2 towards John rather than the reverse. In the former case the sister had requested Jesus' help and addressed him as "Son of David" (1v:24–25). Either for the address or, more likely, for the request, she is "rebuked" by the disciples (1v:25). Then follows, "And Jesus, being angered, went off with her . . . " (1v:25–26). Jesus' anger is explicable here as directed against the disciples and their rebuke of the woman's request. Its presence seems again a mere residue in John.

Garden.   In *SGM* 2 the man's tomb is in "a garden" (1v:26), probably because, as it says later, "he was rich" (2r:6). This is not mentioned in John 11 but in 19:41 the tomb of Jesus is in a "garden." This may be either a facet of its luxury, once again, or even of Edenic resonance, or both. I consider a transfer from *SGM* 2 towards John again more plausible than the reverse.

I consider, therefore, that points such as those, and the full panoply of arguments from sequence, vocabulary, style, and content given by Smith (1973b:97–163), make it much more plausible that John 10:42–11:54 is a greatly expanded and dependent version of *SGM* 2 rather than that *SGM* 2 is a greatly condensed and dependent version of John 10:42–11:54.

Markan Relations

I consider here the general relations between *Secret* Mark and canonical Mark and the particular relations between *SGM* 4–5 and Mark 10:46 Those between *SGM* 2 and canonical Mark will be considered in detail in Case Study 4 below.

Secret Mark and Canonical Mark.   Smith made a very detailed comparison of the vocabulary, phraseology, and grammar of *Secret Mark* and the intracanonical gospels. He concluded that "it is so predominantly Markan that it must be explained as a result either of the same stream of tradition which produced Mk., or of deliberate imitation of Mk." (1973b: 129, 131). I shall code those two explanations as *tradition,* that is a common stream for both *Secret Mark* and canonical Mark, and *imitation*, that is a deliberate modelling of *Secret Mark* on canonical Mark. Smith also compared longer and more specific expressions in *Secret Mark* and the intracanonical gospels and came to the same conclusion. "The evidence from the major parallels confirms that from the minor stylistic traits: it points almost always to Mk. as the source of the material, shows no strong reason to suppose knowledge of any other Gospel, and leaves the alternatives still open—either a free composition by the same school of tradition which produced canonical Mk., or an early imitation of material now found in the canonical Gospel" (1973b:138). Both those explanations, common *tradition* or deliberate *imitation*, could accept Clement's sequence of *Public Mark*, that is, canonical Mark, followed at a later stage by *Secret Mark*. But Smith himself noted that "rereading this text in 1970, more than seven years after it was written and four years after its revision ... I notice that I have not considered the likelihood that Clement, who had no reason to love the secret Gospel, might have been inclined to prefer an account representing it as a secondary expansion of the shorter text which in his day was well on its way to becoming 'canonical'" (1973b: 194).

In 1983 Helmut Koester proposed a very complicated trajectory for the Markan gospel from which I wish here to take only one element. He concluded that "Canonical Mark is derived from Secret Mark. The basic difference between the two seems to be that the redactor of canonical Mark eliminated the story of the raising of the youth and reference to this story in Mk 10:46 ... Clement of Alexandria believed that Mark first wrote the 'canonical' (or 'public') Gospel, and later produced the 'secret' version of this writing. My observations, however, lead to the conclusion that 'canonical' Mark was a purified version of the 'secret' Gospel, because the traces of the author of Secret Mark are still visible in the canonical Gospel of Mark" (1983:56–57).

There are, then, three suggested solutions to the very particular relations between canonical Mark and *Secret Mark,* as outlined in Figure 2.

Figure 2

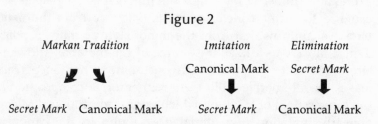

My own working hypothesis is that third possibility. I consider that canonical Mark is a very deliberate revision of *Secret Mark.* It is now impossible to tell the full scope of that revision but two features seem certain. First, canonical Mark eliminated both *SGM* 2 and 5 as discrete literary units. Second, canonical Mark scattered the dismembered elements of those units throughout his gospel. The reason for this elimination was most likely past Carpocratian usage. The reason for this dismembered retention was to offset future Carpocratian usage. Once canonical Mark was accepted, *SGM* 2 and 5 would thereafter read like units composed from words, phrases, and expressions of that gospel. Whether Clement actually knew that *Public/* canonical Mark came second rather than first may be left politely moot.

But how exactly can one decide between *imitation* and *elimination,* between *Secret Mark* having composed units from scattered elements in Mark or Mark having decomposed *Secret Mark* into scattered elements throughout his writing? My basic reason for adopting *elimination* is that those dismembered elements have always caused difficulties for readers of Mark. They do not really fit into their present positions and they have caused incessant problems for ancient readers, such as Matthew and Luke, and for modern interpreters as well.

SGM 4–5 and Mark 10:46. The case study below will be

concerned with *SGM* 1-2-3 and canonical Mark, so I shall not discuss them here. But what of *SGM* 4-5 and canonical Mark?

Clement says that "after the words, 'And he comes into Jericho,' the secret Gospel adds only, 'And the sister of the youth whom Jesus loved and his mother and Salome were there, and Jesus did not receive them'" (2r:14-16). Put kindly, that is mysterious; put unkindly, that is suspicious. I agree completely with Smith's analysis: "Clement uses the verb [receive] often in the cognate sense, 'approve of' a person—that is, of what he says or does . . . —almost 'accept as communicants.' . . . The story, as Clement quotes it, is quite unlike any other NT story because it has no apparently significant content. There is no miracle, no saying, nothing but Jesus' refusal to receive, on one occasion, three women. . . . The original text must have gone on to report some action or saying of Jesus. . . . Most likely it was a conversation with Salome" (1973b:121-22). Either, then, *SGM* 5 had already been expurgated of its content before Clement read it, or Clement is, in this case, extending his programmatic and creative mendacity to poor Theodore himself. In either case, something has been omitted from *SGM* 5.

When SGM 4 is compared with Mark 10:46 there are two important items. First, Clement's quotation in *SGM* 4, "'And he comes into Jericho,'" is the only time his citations differ in any way from our text of canonical Mark. Thus, *SGM* 1 is verbatim the first eight words of Mark 10:32 and verbatim the last four words of 10:34; *SGM* 3 is verbatim the first six words of Mark 10:35; and *SGM* 4 is verbatim the first four words of Mark 10:46, *with one exception*. His quotation here is in the singular, "he comes," but Mark 10:46 has, "And they came to Jericho; and as he was leaving Jericho with his disciples and a great multitude . . ." That reads as if Mark took a singular ("he") and pluralized it before ("they") and after ("with his disciples"). Second, and even more significant, is the effect of something having been omitted between Mark 10:46a, "And they came to Jericho," and 10:46b, "And as he was leaving Jericho." I conclude that Mark

10:46 knew a more original text in which there was mention of something which happened to Jesus at Jericho. But that means that Mark 10:46 is an even more expurgated version of that censored event than is present in *SGM* 5. In other words, Mark 10:46 is a condensed and dependent version of *SGM* 5 rather than *SGM* 5 being an expanded and dependent version of Mark 10:46.

Notice also one very curious feature which will be of significance later on. *SGM* 5 speaks of "the youth whom Jesus loved . . . and Salome." In Mark 10:20–21 the rich man says to Jesus, "'all these I have observed from my youth.' And Jesus looking upon him loved him." Has Mark not only omitted this *SGM* 5 section but dismembered its most dangerous element and used it elsewhere? And has "Salome" from the erased *SGM* 2 found her way to final position in the list of women at Mark 15:40 and 16:1, which is her only mention in the entire New Testament. An affirmative answer to those two questions will be more convincing after the case study below.

So far, therefore, and before the case study to follow, I consider that *SGM* 2 is independent of John 11 and *SGM* 5 is independent of Mark 10:46. Dependence, in fact, is in the opposite direction, from *Secret Mark* to John and Mark.

7 CASE STUDY 4
THE RESURRECTED YOUTH

THE MIRACLE IN SGM 2 AND MARK

Clement says that in between Mark 10:32–34 and 10:35 there appears the following unit, designated here as *SGM* 2 (1v:23–2r:11). It has five literary elements: *Arrival, Request, Miracle, Instruction, Departure.* In giving the text I shall italicize the more obvious phrases which Mark dismembers and relocates and which I shall discuss below:

> And they come into *Bethany.* And a certain woman whose brother had died was there. And, coming, she prostrated herself before Jesus and says to him, *"Son of David, have mercy on me." But the disciples rebuked her.* And Jesus, being angered, went off with her into the garden where the tomb was, and straightway a great cry was heard from the tomb. And going near Jesus *rolled away the stone from the door of the tomb.* And straightway, going in where the *youth* was, he stretched forth his hand and *raised him, seizing his hand.* But the youth, looking upon him, loved him and began to beseech him *that he might be with him.* And going out of the tomb they came into the house of the youth, *for he was rich.* And *after six days* Jesus told him what to do and in the evening the *youth* comes to him, *wearing a linen cloth over his naked body.* And he remained with him that night, for Jesus taught him the *mystery of the kingdom of God.* And thence, arising, he returned to the *other side of the Jordan.*

My point is that canonical Mark took the phrases and expressions of that story, both small and large, and scattered them over the rest of the gospel. This can be proved more easily with the larger expresssions, of course. With the smaller ones, one might argue simple coincidence of subject matter or common speech.

111

Arrival

Mark mentions "Bethany" at 11:1, 11, 12 and has Jesus in a house there at 14:3. That first mention reads, "And when they drew near to Jerusalem, to Bethphage and Bethany, at the Mount of Olives." Mark's awkward relocation of "Bethany" at 11:1 is signalled by rephrasing in Luke 19:28–29, elimination in Matt 21:1.

Request

In *SGM* 2 she beseeches Jesus with, "'Son of David, have mercy on me.' But the disciples rebuked her." This now appears at Mark 10:47–48 where blind Bartimaeus pleads, in very strange word order, "'Son of David, Jesus, have mercy on me!' And many rebuked him, telling him to be silent; but he cried out all the more, 'Son of David, have mercy on me!'" Mark's original story probably read only "Jesus!" since the request comes later after a question from Jesus in 10:51. Mark's awkward combination of the "Son of David" with "Jesus" as "Son of David, Jesus" is signalled by "Son of David" alone in Matt 9:27; 20:30–31, and the more normal "Jesus, Son of David" in Luke 18:38.

Miracle

There are three items worth noting in this section: the stone, the youth, the hand.

Stone. The phrase "rolled away the stone from the door of the tomb" from *SGM* 2 is relocated to Mark 16:3 where the women on their way to Jesus' tomb "were saying to one another, 'Who will roll away the stone for us from the door of the tomb?' And looking up, they saw that the stone was rolled back." Neither Matt 28:2 nor Luke 24:2 find the women's comment worth copying but it does exactly what Mark intended.

Youth. In *SGM* 2 the one in the tomb is a *neaniskos*, a youth or young man. And Jesus enters the tomb himself, "going in where the youth was." If that seems an obvious act, note how

John 11:43 keeps Jesus always outside the tomb. Mark relocates this to 16:5 where the women "entering the tomb . . . saw a young man." Once again, the other Synoptic writers change this. Luke 24:4 has "behold two men" as in his Transfiguration (Luke 9:30) and Ascension (Acts 1:10) scenes, but the women do enter the tomb. Matt 28:2 has an "angel" and all takes place outside the tomb.

Hand. In *SGM* 2 the miracle happens as Jesus "raised him, seizing his hand." Mark uses this almost as a stock phrase, in 1:31; 5:41; 9:27. Of those three instances, the phrase is retained only in Mark 5:41 = Matt 9:25 = Luke 8:54; it is omitted at Mark 1:31 = Matt 8:15 = Luke 4:39 and Mark 9:27 = Matt 17:18 = Luke 9:42.

A footnote. That last instance involves the cure of *The Epileptic Boy.* Mark 9:21 records that he has been possessed "since childhood," which leaves his age deliberately vague. And Mark 9:26 says that "the boy was like a corpse, so that most of them said, 'He is dead.'" Both Matt 17:18 and Luke 9:42 lack those two comments. I propose that Mark redacted this story with traces from the eliminated story of *The Resurrected Youth* in *SGM* 2 as part of the same process of dismemberment and redistribution. It need hardly be stressed how many warning comments Mark makes in this story: see 9:18–19, 23–24, 28–29 on faith and prayer, as against, what? Magic, maybe, or spell?

Instruction

There are six points to be noted here: youth-love-rich, beseech, house, six days, naked at night, mystery of the kingdom.

Youth-Love-Rich. In *SGM* 2 "the youth, looking upon him, loved him . . . he was rich." Mark removes those three notes to the story of *The Rich Man* in 10:17–22 but changes them somewhat in the transfer. The "youth" is not exactly that any longer since he kept the commandments "from his youth." Now, Jesus "looking upon him loved him," rather than the reverse. And, after he is told to give all to the poor, "his countenance fell, and he went away sorrowful; for he had great possessions." In other words, there was originally no linkage whatsoever between the story of *The Rich Man* in Mark 10:17–22 and the story of *The Resurrected Youth* in *SGM* 2. I have two arguments for this position. One is from *Secret Mark* and one is from Clement. (1) In *SGM* 2 the youth to be resurrected is introduced like this: "And they come to Bethany. And a certain woman whose brother had died was there." I do not think a youth so introduced was known to the narrative already. (2) Clement wrote a short treatise specifically on Mark 10:17–31 called *The Rich Man's Salvation* (Butterworth: 270–367) to reassure well-to-do Christians about their destiny. Had he known a linked narrative about a rich young man who was invited but refused, and then resurrected and baptized, I cannot comprehend his not using it in that homily. If one objects that the linkage was part of secret baptismal liturgy, then his converts would probably not have needed that homily. I wish to underline this point. *SGM* 2 was most likely part of an Alexandrian baptismal reading and ritual, as Clement seems to claim: "it even yet is most carefully guarded, being read only to those who are being initiated into the great mysteries" (1v:1–2). But I do not think that rich Alexandrians were assured at their baptism that *The Rich Man* who first refused Jesus was the same as *The Resurrected Youth* who belatedly accepted him. My objection, of course, is only to the linkage, to the equation of *The Rich Man* and *The Resurrected Youth* which I consider were originally quite separate and discrete incidents. It is Mark who "linked" them by dismemberment, relocation, and rephrasing of the elements from *SGM* 2 back into Mark 10:17–22. Smith proposed that "the details of Mk. 10:13–34 + the longer text + 10.35–45 show the whole pericope to be a baptismal lection, to which all its parts are essential" (1973b:187). This is most probably correct, but the equation of the characters in Mark 10:17–22 and *SGM* 2 was never present before canonical Mark went to work on that latter text.

Another footnote. Mark 10:20 has "from my youth," which is accepted by Luke 18:21 but changed to "the young man (*neaniskos*) said" in Matt 19:20. And while Mark 10:22 has "he had great possessions," which is retained by Matt 19:22, it appears as "he was very rich" in Luke 18:23. Both "young man" and "rich" are terms from *SGM* 2. How is this to be explained? If Matt 19:16–22 and Luke 18:18–23 are here following Mark 10:17–22, how are they closer to *SGM* 2 on these two points? I consider both those points to be well within tolerable coincidence and presume no separate knowledge of *Secret Mark* by Matthew and Luke. I would be more surprised if both Matthew and Luke had the same two differences rather than each having one which the other did not. On the one hand, Matt 19:20 made an obvious change since "rich young man" was a better warning and the fact that the story's title was thereafter taken from his text rather than Mark's or Luke's confirms his judgment. On the other, "rich" appears in the Markan context at 10:25, and is also a typical term for Luke.

Beseech. The phrase "began to beseech him that he might be with him" in *SGM* 2 is relocated by canonical Mark to 5:18 where the cured demoniac "begged him that he might be with him." Matt 8:34 totally omits this, and Luke 8:38, who retains it, completely rephrases it in Greek.

House. In *SGM* 2 "they came into the house of the youth." In Mark 1:16 Jesus calls "Simon and Andrew . . . James . . . and John"; then in 1:29 he goes to "the house of Simon and Andrew, with James and John." In 2:14 he calls Levi and in 2:15 he is in his house. In 3:13–19 he chooses the Twelve and in 3:20 he is in a house. There are no problems with those first two examples in Mark 1:29 = Matt 8:14 = Luke 4:8 and Mark 2:15 = Matt 9:10 = Luke 5:29. But that third and rather forced case is omitted completely by Matthew and Luke. Mark intends to set up a rhythm of calling/visiting so that the case in *SGM* 2 is no longer anything particularly special.

Six Days. *SGM* 2 has "after six days," and this may be of some significance for baptismal preparation in the Alexandrian church. Thomas J. Talley finds in this text the best explanation for the fact that "a peculiar aspect of the Coptic tradition is that it identifies the baptismal day, the sixth day of the sixth week, with a tradition which asserted that that day was the day on which Jesus baptized his disciples" (44). This chronological item is now relocated to Mark 9:2 where one can only describe it as not exactly clear. Matt 17:1 accepts it there but Luke 9:28 changes it to "about eight days."

Naked at Night. This is, of course, by far the most important element in the entire discussion. *SGM* 2 says that "in the evening the youth comes to him, wearing a linen cloth over his naked body." This is now in Mark 14:51–52 where, in the garden of Gethsemane, "A young man followed him, with nothing but a linen cloth about his body; and they seized him, but he left the linen cloth and ran away naked." Matt 26:56 and Luke 22:53 have no such incident. What is the meaning of this nocturnal encounter in *SGM* 2?

1) Naked Baptism. In the first part we saw the combination of wisdom speculation, paradise regained, and sexual asceticism that was constitutive of Thomistic theology. This can now be specified in further detail. Gen 2:25 says that "the man and his wife were both naked, and were not ashamed," but, after their fall, Gen 3:7 notes that "the eyes of both were opened, and they knew that they were naked; and they sewed fig leaves together and made themselves aprons." Later, after their condemnation, Gen 3:21 records that "the Lord God made for Adam and for his wife garments of skins, and clothed them." There are two texts in *Thomas* which indicate how baptismal ritual reversed this sequence. They are both in question and answer format. In *Gos. Thom* 21: "Mary said to Jesus, 'Whom are your disciples like?' He said, 'They are like children who have settled in a field which is not theirs. When the owners of the field come, they will say, 'Let us have back our field. They (will) undress in their presence in order to let them have back their

field and to give it back to them.'" And in *Gos. Thom.* 37: "His disciples said, 'When will You become revealed to us and when shall we see You?' Jesus said, 'When you disrobe without being ashamed and take up your garments and place them under your feet like little children and tread on them, then [will you see] the Son of the Living One, and you will not be afraid.'" Jonathan Z. Smith has shown quite brilliantly that "the origin of logion 37 is to be found within archaic Christian baptismal practices and attendant interpretation of Genesis 1–3" and that "the four principal motifs within the logion—the undressing of the disciples, their being naked and without shame, their treading upon the garments, and their being as little children— are to be found joined together only within baptismal rituals and homilies. The nudity of the initiant—a feature shared by early Christianity with the initiation rites of the Hellenistic Mysteries and Jewish proselyte 'baptism' was found to be consistently related to the symbolism of new life or birth" (218, 237). Wayne A. Meeks says of the Pauline tradition that "there can be little doubt that the 'taking off' and 'putting on' is first of all an interpretation of the act of disrobing, which must have preceded baptism, and of the dressing afterward" and he coments that "disrobing before baptism is explicitly mentioned or presupposed in the earliest complete baptismal rituals known to us, as well as in the earliest paintings of baptism in catacomb art" (183).

2) Night Baptism. In John 3:2 Nicodemus comes to Jesus "by night" and there is talk, but here no more, about baptism. And, accident or not, baptism is nocturnal in Acts 16:33. And, as Morton Smith, notes, Hippolytus of Rome, who died about 235, records in *Apostolic Tradition* XXI that baptism is nude and at dawn after a nocturnal vigil (1973b:175).

There is, therefore, nothing in any way out of the ordinary in *SGM* 2, taken in itself and against this general early baptismal liturgy. Jesus takes the resurrected youth through a nude and nocturnal baptism and this incident could easily have been read as individuals were being so baptized in Alexandrian ritual. It seems, however, that the Carpocratians read this scene in terms of erotic rather than Edenic symbolism and either added or interpreted "naked man with naked man" (2r:13) so that the whole took on a homosexual implication. I find, however, that there is no more *intrinsic* prurience here than in John 3:2 or *Gos. Thom.* 21 and 37. I see no evidence that Jesus and the youth are engaged in anything shocking. And I prefer to let the Carpocratians alone in salivating over the incident. But once they had done so, one can understand the solution adopted by canonical Mark in relocating the unit to 14:51–52 and letting future readers worry over what it might mean. He himself may possibly have seen it now as symbolic of Jesus who would escape his captors leaving behind but a linen cloth in the tomb.

Mystery of the Kingdom. The baptismal instruction in *SGM* 2 involved "the mystery of the kingdom of God." Mark relocates this to 4:11 and tells the disciples, "To you has been given the secret [mystery] of the kingdom of God." Both Matt 13:11 and Luke 8:9 change this into a more expected format: "to know the secrets [mysteries] of the kingdom." A plural "mysteries" is also found in 1 Cor 4:1; 13:2; 14:2; *Gos. Thom.* 62. You will recall, however, that the final quotation from Irenaeus' *Against Heresies* given above, cited the Carpocratians as "declaring that Jesus spoke in a mystery to his disciples and apostles privately" 1.25.5; *ANF:* 1.96). Mark has safely neutralized this assertion by situating the instruction not within secret ritual but after public parable.

Departure

After the nocturnal baptism *SGM* 2 says of Jesus that, "thence, arising, he returned to the other side (*peran*) of the Jordan." In Mark 10:1 there is a strange geographical note: "And he left there [literally: thence, arising] and went to the region of Judea and beyond (*peran*) the Jordan." Luke 9:51 ignores this strange conjunction and Matt 19:1 changes it to "Judea beyond the Jordan." But for Mark it was a simple question of storing some *SGM* debris somewhere safe.

THE MIRACLE IN TRADITION
Transmission

This is surely one of the most complicated cases imaginable. I am not convinced, however, that you can plausibly explain *Secret Mark* as a drastically summarized version of John 11 written in deliberate Markan or Synoptic terms and phrases (Brown). But neither am I convinced that it is necessary to propose an earlier Proto-Mark gospel which was first used in different versions by Luke and Matthew and then developed into *Secret Mark* and *Carpocratian Mark* before being purified as *Public*/canonical Mark (Koester, 1983:54–57).

My own solution presumes three major stages. (1) First, there was the common source for *SGM* 2 and John 11. Whether this was a single miracle-story, an aretalogy of miraculous deeds, or even the gospel of a miracle-working Jesus can now only be conjectured. (2) Second, there was the Markan tradition. The linguistic and stylistic affinities between *Secret Mark* and *Public*/canonical Mark demand a common author, group, or school at the root of this process. This second stage has three subsidiary moments. (2a) In the beginning was *SGM*. This included at least Mark 10:32–34 + *SGM* 2 + Mark 10:35–46a + *SGM* 5 + some incident at Jericho. It is no longer possible to know how much else it contained before and after those units. It is at least possible that it concluded with the post-baptismal encounter between Jesus and the resurrected youth at Jericho. In any case, I do not *presume* it contained a passion and resurrection conclusion. This *Secret Mark* which caused all the controversy, was most likely used as baptismal reading and ritual in the Alexandrian church. (2b) *Secret Mark* was possibly interpolated

119

and certainly interpreted in *Carpocratian Mark*. This turned the Edenic symbolism of normal naked baptism into erotic and homosexual antinomianism in the tradition of Gnostic libertinism. (2c) In order to eliminate the Carpocratian scandal and redeem *Secret Mark* for catholicism, this final version, our canonical Mark, carefully dismembered *SGM* 2 and 5 and distributed the textual debris at various locations in the gospel. I do not presume that this was the only reason for the composition of canonical Mark but I think either the same author or school produced both the original *Secret Mark* and the anti-Carpocratian *Public*/canonical Mark. The purpose is magnificently clear. After canonical Mark was present, it would be simple to accuse the Carpocratians of having manufactured their version by culling terms and phrases, bits and pieces from Mark. The key argument for my interpretation here is how those dismembered fragments have kept ancient and modern interpreters puzzling over their meaning in canonical Mark. (3) Third, there is the Synoptic reaction. When Matthew and Luke come to use canonical Mark, they found difficulties with those fragments just as they did with many other themes and topics in Markan theology. Their separate and individual or even common and coincidental changes on those dismembered fragments do not demand any special knowledge of *Secret Mark* on their part or any usage of radically divergent versions of canonical Mark. The Two Source theory presumes and finds acceptable the major coincidence that, separately and independently, Matthew and Luke considered Mark needed rewriting. After that major coincidence on rewriting, minor coincidences in rewriting were inevitable.

Clement, unfortunately for him, wanted to have it both ways, wanted to have both the canonical and secret versions of Mark. This leaves him very vulnerable to a text such as the Carpocratian version or interpretation of Mark. This letter gives the best explanation he can come up with for the three versions.

Intertextuality

In the first part, and in both its case studies, the text of Christian history infiltrated and controlled the recitation and interpretation of the parables of *The Great Supper* and *The Evil Tenants*. In the present case there is an even stranger intertextuality at play. The text of the Carpocratian reading and practice of *Secret Mark* rendered it necessary to eliminate certain sections from that gospel. These were eliminated by dismemberment and redistribution so that the Carpocratian reading would ever after seem a collage of those dispersed bits and pieces. Thus *Carpocratian Mark* is controlling the way *Secret Mark* will finally become *Public*/canonical Mark. Intertextuality, then, can have a negative just as well as a positive effect.

Part Four

THE GOSPEL OF PETER

I don't know what happened to the *Gospel of Peter* between, say, the first or second century when it was originally written, and the time when it was copied as an amulet in the eighth century and put into the tomb of a Christian monk. That makes it very difficult because, for one thing, the canonical Gospels were fairly well treated after the third century ... I think we have to do text-critical work on the *Gospel of Peter*. One cannot just say this must have been a gospel from the first century; one would have to sit down and say, now, what is late and what is early.

(Koester, 1983:82)

8 THE GOSPEL OF PETER INTRODUCTION

The opening seminar for the "Colloquy on New Testament Studies" at Southwestern Baptist Theological Seminary in November of 1980 concerned a paper by Helmut Koester which I have already mentioned. During the seminar dialogue after his paper, Koester made the above comments on the *Gospel of Peter*. This final part will suggest answers to the problems and questions proposed in those comments.

DISCOVERY

In the case of the *Gospel of Thomas*, Greek fragments had been discovered at Oxyrhynchus a half century before a full Coptic version was unearthed at Nag Hammadi. The present situation is similar but more complicated because no complete version of the *Gospel of Peter* has yet been discovered.

The Gospel of Peter in the Akhmim Codex

In discussing Nag Hammadi in the first part, I mentioned the earlier monastic foundations of St. Pachomius at Chenoboskia and Pabau on the east bank of the Nile nearby. Akhmim, the ancient Panopolis, over sixty miles north along the river and also on the east bank, was the site of a third Pachomian monastery.

"An extensive Christian necropolis, begun in the fifth century, bears witness to the ecclesiastical importance of the place in days before the Arab invasion . . . during the winter of 1886–87 the researches of the French Archeological Mission in Egypt led to the discovery in one of the graves of Christian Panopolis of a small book measuring 6 inches by 4, and containing 33 leaves of parchment, stitched together into covers of pasteboard roughly cased in leather" (Swete: xlv). The codex, now in the Cairo Museum, contained extracts in Greek from four different texts: (1) the *Gospel of Peter*, (2) the *Apocalypse of Peter*, (3) *1 Enoch* 1:1–32:6; and (4) the *Acts of St. Julian* represented by a single page pasted inside the back cover.

The first recto of the manuscript is blank save for decoration. This consists of a large cross, alpha and omega below the bar, two smaller crosses at the extremities above the bar, and the entire design within a square (Lods: Plate II). The manuscript is in very good condition with but slight damage from moisture and insects on the first pages.

> Enoch and the fragment of the Acts . . . [are] in uncial characters which appear to be those of the seventh or eighth century; the Petrine fragments are written in a cursive script of a peculiar type, probably belonging to the same period. It is worthy of notice that while each of the Petrine fragments is followed by a blank, as if the writer had stopped because he had reached the end of his copy, there is no such blank between the fragments of the Enoch or at the end of the Codex. It would seem as if the writer of the Petrine matter having in his possession some leaves of Enoch which were nearly of the same size with his 'Peter,' bound the whole together. At the death of the writer (or of the last owner of the book, if it fell into other hands) the precious collection was buried with him. From the position of the grave, M. Bouriant infers that the burial took place not before the beginning of the eighth century, nor after the end of the twelfth (Swete: xlvi).

The extract from the *Gospel of Peter* begins on the verso of the decorated first page and covers folios 1v–5v, pages 2–10 (Bouriant; Lods). Although it opens in the middle of an incident it has the initial decoration of a small cross at the top of its first page. And, although it stops in the middle of a sentence it has the terminal decoration of three small crosses and an ornamental band on its last page. Also, although all the preceding pages had from seventeen to nineteen lines apiece, that last page has

126

only fourteen. The presumption is that the version from which the copyist worked was already fragmentary. We cannot tell, therefore, the complete content or even nature of this *Gospel of Peter*.

The Gospel of Peter in the Oxyrhynchus Papyri

In 1972 R. A. Coles edited what he described as "fragments of an apocryphal gospel(?)" which had been discovered among the Oxyrhynchus Papyri (Browne: 15–16; see Plate II). These two tiny fragments, today in Oxford's Ashmolean Museum, measure about three by one and a half inches and one by a half inch. "The larger fragment covered thirteen lines, but the surface at ll. 2 and 4 is now entirely abraded. No margins are preserved. The smaller fragment (2) has the beginnings of five lines, and probably should be placed to the lower left of (1), but as regards the precise line-alignment neither fibres nor text seem conclusive, nor has the use of a light-table been helpful. The verso is blank; the book therefore was apparently not a codex" (Browne: 15). Coles described the handwriting as "an informal slanting type . . . I would assign it to the early third or possibly late second century." Of the content, he said that, "the larger of these fragments relates the story of Joseph of Arimathaea's request to Pilate for the body of Jesus, in a version which is not that of the canonical Gospels. Among the Apocrypha its closest resemblances are to the Gospel of Peter, #2, although even from this it has considerable variations" (Browne: 15).

DATE

Coles peruasively aligned Oxy P 2949, fragment 1, lines 5–12, with the Akhmim Fragment of the *Gospel of Peter* 2:3–5a. The most important common item is the very unusual phrase "friend of Pilate" found in both texts. He also suggested, but somewhat less persuasively, that Oxy P 2949, fragment 2, lines

127

15–17, should be aligned with the *Gospel of Peter* 2:5b. This is possible but more problematic (see Lührmann). In any case, the evidence from fragment 1 alone is enough to push the date for this text back six hundred years from the eighth or ninth to the second or third centuries. There is one very interesting result from this dating. The first two Christian manuscripts we have, dating from the early second century, are Papyrus 52 of John and Egerton Papyrus 2, that is, one intra- and one extracanonical text. The next earliest ones we have, dating to the late second or early third centuries, are Papyri 64+67 for Matthew, Papyrus 66 for John, and Oxy P 1 for the *Gospel of Thomas*, Oxy P 2949 for the *Gospel of Peter*. Once again there is a balance of intra- and extracanonical texts (see Koester, 1980:107–11). It seems that the dry sands of Egypt have little regard for questions of canonicity.

Titles such as Oxy P 2949, the Akhmim Fragment, or even Codex Panopolitanus, are all neutral terms, more descriptive of whence than of what. Why, then, the title *Gospel of Peter*?

Gos. Pet. 7:26–27 says, "But I mourned with my fellows, and being wounded in heart we hid ourselves, for we were sought after by them as evildoers and as persons who wanted to set fire to the temple. Because of all these things we were fasting and sat mourning and weeping night and day until the sabbath." A similar comment is made in *Gos. Pet.* 14:59–60 but here the identity of the writer is given: "But we, the twelve disciples of the Lord, wept and mourned, and each one, very grieved for what had come to pass, went to his own home. But I, Simon Peter, and my brother Andrew took our nets and went to the sea." The author is thus identified as Simon Peter.

Oxy P 2949 has pushed the latest date for this *Gospel of Peter* back to the "late second or early third century" (Browne: 15). Is there any other external evidence that might push the *terminus ad quem* back even earlier? The answer is negative. From Swete in 1893 (xxviii-xxxv) to Denker in 1975 (9-30) the conclusion is that there is no clear evidence of usage for this *Gospel of Peter* before the end of the second century. There is, however, one very interesting mention of it at that time.

The case involves Serapion, Bishop of Antioch, and the use of the *Gospel of Peter* in the church at Rhossus. "Serapion's episcopate began betwen A.D. 189 and 192: the year of his death is less certain, but he seems to have been still living during the persecution of the Church by Septimius Severus (A.D. 202–3). On the whole his period of episcopal activity may safely be placed in the last decade of the second century. . . . Rhosus stood just inside the bay of Issus (the modern gulf of Iskendurun); to the southwest, fifty miles off, lay the extremity of the long arm of Cyprus; Antioch was not above thirty miles to the south east, but lofty hills, a continuation of the range of Amanus, prevented direct communication with the capital" (Swete: x-xi). Here is what Eusebius, Bishop of Caesarea, who died in 339 or 340, records about Serapion in his *Ecclesiastical History* 6.12.2–6 (Lake & Oulton: 2.40–43):

> Another book has been composed by him *Concerning what is known as the Gospel of Peter*, which he has written refuting the false statements in it, because of certain in the community of Rhossus, who on the ground of the said writing turned aside into heterodox teachings. It will not be unreasonable to quote a short passage from this work, in which he puts forward the view he held about the book, writing as follows: "For our part, brethren, we receive both Peter and the other apostles as Christ, but the writings which falsely bear their names we reject, as men of experience, knowing that such were not handed down to us. For I myself, when I came among you, imagined that all of you clung to the true faith; and, without going through the Gospel put forward by them in the name of Peter, I said: If this is the only thing that seemingly causes captious feelings among you, let it be read. But since I have now learnt, from what has been told me, that their mind was lurking in some hole of heresy, I shall give diligence to come again to you; wherefore, brethren, expect me quickly. But we, brethren, gathering to what kind of heresy Marcianus belonged (who used to contradict himself, not knowing what he was saying, as ye will learn from what has been written to you), were enabled by others who studied this very Gospel, that is, by the successors of those who

began it, whom we call Docetae (for most of the ideas belong to their
teaching)—using [the material supplied] by them, were enabled to go
through it and discover that the most part indeed was in accordance
with the true teaching of the Saviour, but that some things were
added, which also we place below for your benefit."

Eusebius' account stops at this point without giving any of
Serapion's examples of docetic teachings in the *Gospel of Peter*.

In terms of external evidence, then, the *Gospel of Peter* is
known in an obscure corner of western Syria in the last decade
of the second century and in Oxyrhynchus in Egypt at about
the same or a slightly later period. This means that "the latest
possible date would be in the second half of the second century" (Cameron: 77).

CONTENT

The document was divided into sixty verses by Adolf von
Harnack and into fourteen chapters by J. A. Robinson. Hence it
is usually cited by chapter and verse but each of these run
sequentially throughout the entire text (see *NTA:* 1.183–87;
Cameron: 78–82).

In the three case studies to follow I cover most of the content
of the *Gospel of Peter* so there is no need to outline it in detail
here. In general, however, and for my own convenience in
presentation, I have divided the gospel's content into six major
units and these will be used as titles hereafter. They are given in
Figure 3.

Is the content of this gospel docetic, that is, does it deny the
reality of Jesus' humanity and claim that it was only an
appearance? Recall the multiple ambiguities cited concerning
this gospel in the preceding section: (1) Rhossus was already in
debate over it before Serapion's arrival. (2) Serapion initially
approved its use. (3) Serapion later discovered "some things"
which were docetic in it but only guided by the usage of

Marcianus, who was presumably the leader of the Docetae at Rhossus. (4) Even then, Serapion still found "the most part" of the gospel to be quite orthodox. Recently J. W. McCant has argued convincingly that "the 'Lord' of GP is equivalent to the 'Jesus in the flesh' of the canonical gospels; he is abused, mocked, crucified, tormented and offered a death potion; when he dies, nails are removed from his hands, his body is washed and buried and women come to the tomb expecting to go in and sit down beside the Lord. Certainly such a presentation (almost an exaggerated realism) resists a docetic Christology" (269). There is no doubt, however, that certain phrases in the *Gospel of Peter* could be interpreted docetically and apparently were so read at Rhossus. But then so could certain units in the intracanonical gosepls, especially that of John. One example may suffice. *Gos. Pet.* 4:10 says that on the cross Jesus "held his peace, as if he felt no pain." Is this docetism? In the *Martyrdom of Polycarp* 8:3, the martyr "getting down from the carriage . . . scraped his shin; and without turning round, as though he had suffered nothing, he walked on promptly and quickly, and was taken to the arena" (Lake: 2.323). There is a difference between "as if he felt no pain" and "because he felt no pain." The *Gospel of Peter* does not derive from an essentially docetic vision of the passion although it may well have been so interpreted at Rhossus.

Figure 3

Unit	Narrative Content	Gos. Pet.
GP 1	*Crucifixion and Deposition*	1:1–6:22
GP 2	*Joseph and Burial*	6:23–24
GP 3	*Tomb and Guards*	7:25–9:34
GP 4	*Resurrection and Confession*	9:35–11:49
GP 5	*Women and Youth*	12:50–13:57
GP 6	*Disciples and(?) Apparition*	14:58–60 . . .

INDEPENDENCE

Independence or Dependence?

On the relations between the *Gospel of Peter* and the intra-canonical gospels, scholarship is as split as was the church of Rhossus over its usage and the mind of Serapion over its content. The split was well established by 1893 when Adolf von Harnack argued for independence, except for the possible use of Mark especially in the *Women and Youth* incident, and Theodore Zahn maintained the complete and late dependence of Peter on the other gospels (Johnson: 3–4). It is still evident in the introductions to the English translation of the *Gospel of Peter* most easily available in this country. Christian Maurer describes it as "a further development of the traditional material of the four canonical Gospels. These are used as remembered, whilst the oral transmission of the material in the preaching of the gospel has also told upon it" (*NTA*: 2.180). But Ron Cameron argues, on the contrary, that "the *Gospel of Peter* is an independent witness of gospel traditions . . . it is quite possible that the document as we have it antedates the four gospels of the New Testament and may have served as a source for their respective authors" (78).

Helmut Koester has also argued forcibly for the independent status of the *Gospel of Peter*. On the *Crucifixion and Deposition* unit he claimed that it was "an independent witness of the formation of the passion narrative." And on the *Resurrection and Confession* incident he noted that "various parts of this story are in fact preserved in the canonical gospels; however, they have been inserted into different contexts and are fragments of an older story that only the *Gospel of Peter* has preserved intact" (1980:128,129). His choice of those two units as examples of independence should be underlined for future reference, as also should his statements quoted as epigraph to this part.

Independence and Dependence

My own position will be worked out in detail during the three case studies to follow. This is just a general overview of the proposed solution. It explains, among other things, the ambiguous status of the *Gospel of Peter*, all the way from the second to the twentieth century.

1. The *Gospel of Peter* contains three units which are independent of the intracanonical gospels and where, indeed, the dependence is in the opposite direction. These three units formed a linked and self-consistent complex which I call the Passion-Resurrection Source and which was used by all four of our intracanonical gospels. Its three units are:

> (a) *GP 1: Crucifixion and Deposition* (1:1–6:22)
> (b) *GP 3: Tomb and Guards* (7:25–9:34)
> (c) *GP 4: Resurrection and Confession* (9:35–11:49).

2. The *Gospel of Peter* also contains three units which are dependent on and directly derived from the intracanonical gospels. These three units are:

> (a) *GP 2: Joseph and Burial* (6:23–24)
> (b) *GP 5: Women and Youth* (12:50–13:57)
> (c) *GP 6: Disciples and(?) Apparition* (14:58–60 . . .)

3. The *Gospel of Peter* is composed by a careful integration of those two triads into one another and by the attribution of the entire product to Simon Peter. This integration is effected by having "previews" of the later and dependent units inserted into the earlier and independent ones. These preparatory previews will not be discussed here but will be studied in the cases to follow.

I see, therefore, at least two major stages in the composition of the *Gospel of Peter*. A first stage involved *GP 1-3-4* as a coherent and self-contained unit, that is, the Passion-Resurrection Source. A second stage combined *GP 2-5-6* with this earlier complex and then, strictly speaking, it became for the first time the pseudepigraphical work of Peter. I do not think that the Passion-Resurrection Source was attributed in any way to Peter. I would insist that this overall conflation is more than a simple juxtaposition of units. The final composition went out of its way to integrate old and new, earlier and later sections, and to bring all under the authorship and authority of Peter. This is summarized in Figure 4.

Figure 4

Independent Tradition	Redactional Preparation	Dependent Tradition
GP 1 (1:1–6:22)	with 2:3–5a for	*GP 2* (6:23–24)
GP 3 (7:25–9:34)	with 7:26–27 for	*GP 6* (14:58–60)
GP 4 (9:35–11:49)	with 9:37 & 11:43–44 for	*GP 5* (12:50–13:57)

Composition and Authority

Before turning to the case studies, two footnotes may be added to that overall solution.

First, I have described *Gos. Pet.* 2:3–5a as "redactional preparation" between older tradition independent of the intracanonical gospels and later tradition dependent on those gospels. But it was precisely 2:3–5a which was present in Oxy P 2949, fragment 1, lines 5–12. Therefore, I presume that as far back as we have external evidence, we are dealing with this integrated composition and not just with its earlier and independent sections. The *Gospel of Peter* is that integrated composition pseudepigraphically attributed to Peter. No wonder Rhossus and Serapion had troubles with the text!

Second, I would add not a proof that this composition did happen but an analogy which shows that the composition could happen. It also shows that it could happen relatively early in the second century. This is the case of John's gospel. In both the *Gospel of Peter* and of John we seem to have (1) a mingling of traditions both independent and dependent on the Synoptic gospels, (2) integrated smoothly and carefully, (3) in the environment of western Syria, and (4) showing concern for the authority or even primacy of Simon Peter. I do not want to go too far into this analogy here but I note one point. The debate over whether John is independent or dependent on the Synoptics has to be answered not with either/or but both/and. This is not just inept compromise but an attempt to face all the evidence simultaneously. Thus D. Moody Smith concludes a very careful review of all the arguments on this subject by admitting that "I am beginning to be able to conceive of a scenario in which John knew, or knew of, the synoptics and yet produced so dissimilar a gospel as the one which now follows them in the New Testament. . . . In this community an independent tradition of Jesus' miracles, especially healings, has circulated (perhaps a *semeia*-source), and such tradition of his logia as has existed has been subjected to thorough-going reinterpretation. . . . The influence of the synoptics was at best secondary and perhaps in some cases even second-hand" (443). Thus, in ways that still need more precise description, an originally independent Johannine tradition has been merged with elements dependent on the Synoptic gospels. So too, and in ways that also need more precise description, the originally independent Passion-Resurrection Source was eventually merged with the intracanonical gospels.

9 CASE STUDY 5 PROPHECY AND PASSION

This will concern *GP 1: Crucifixion and Deposition* (1:1–6:22) but ignore the preparatory insert for *GP 2: Joseph and Burial* (6:23–24) in 2:3–5a.

The main parallels between this unit in *Peter* and in the intracanonical gospels are given in Figure 5. I shall refer to these elements by number and name hereafter.

Figure 5

Literary Elements	*Peter*	Matthew	Mark	Luke	John
1 Hand Washing	1:1	27:24a			
2 Herod's Role	1:1,2			23:6–12	
3 Jesus Handed Over	2:5b	27:26b	15:15b	23:25b	19:16
4 Eve of Passover	2:5b				19:14
5 Mockery	3:6–9	27:27–31	15:16–20		19:2–3
6 Between Criminals	4:10	27:38	15:27	23:33b	19:18
7 Superscription	4:11	27:37	15:26	23:38	19:19
8 Garments by Lot	4:12	27:35	15:24	23:34b	
9 Criminal Confesses	4:13			23:39–43	
10 Legs Unbroken	4:14				19:31–37
11 Darkness Starts	5:15	27:45a	15:33a	23:44a	
12 Gall & Vinegar	5:16–17	27:34	15:23		
		27:48	15:36	23:36	19:28–29
13 Darkness Stays	5:18				
14 Cry of Jesus	5:19a	27:46	15:34		
15 Jesus Dies	5:19b	27:50	15:37	23:46	19:30
16 Temple Veil Rent	5:20	27:51a	15:38		
17 Deposition & Quake	6:21	27:51b			
18 Darkness Ends	6:22	27:45b	15:33b	23:44b	

I do not intend to study all those parallels in arguing that *GP 1: Crucifixion and Deposition* is not dependent on the intra-canonical gospels but, rather, that those four are dependent on it. Fuller and more detailed arguments for this thesis are already available, from Gardner-Smith (1925–26a) to Denker (1975).

My selection of elements for analysis is dictated by five important aspects of that comparative table: (1) Certain elements are common to all five gospels: Nos. 3, 6, 7, 12, 15. (2) There is no element found only in *Peter* and in Mark. (3) There are two elements found only in *Peter* and in Matthew: Nos. 1, 17. (4) There are two elements found only in *Peter* and in Luke: Nos. 2, 9. (5) There are two elements found only in *Peter* and in John: Nos. 4, 10.

THE PASSION IN THE FIVE GOSPELS

In his 1972 Kiel dissertation, Jürgen Denker has shown (58–77) in very great detail the tissue of resonances especially from Isaiah and the Psalms which lies beneath the narrative of the passion in Peter. Helmut Koester agrees that, "The passion narrative of the *Gospel of Peter* is indeed written, sentence for sentence, in the spirit of this 'scriptural memory.' It is closely related to the teaching and preaching of the earliest Christian communities where the passion of Jesus from the very beginning was probably never told without the framework of such scriptural reference. The canonical gospels, on the other hand, show an increasing historicizing interest, add martyrological features, and want more precisely to demonstrate, in apologetic fashion, the correspondence between prophecy and fulfilment" (1980:127–28). As an illustration of this pervasive process, I choose one element (No. 12) from those common to all five gospels.

Psalm 69:21 (68:22 in LXX) says: "They gave me poison [gall] for food, and for my thirst they gave me vinegar to drink."

Those two elements appear in close conjunction in the pseudo-letter of pseudo-Barnabas, a treatise on the allegorical interpretation of the Old Testament, dating from the late first or early second century. *Barn.* 7:3 says that when Jesus "was crucified he was given to drink vinegar and gall," and in 7:5, "you are going to give to me gall and vinegar to drink." That last verse, literally, "gall with vinegar," is the same as in *Gos. Pet.* 5:16, and it indicates how early this biblical allusion is. Both *Barnabas* and *Peter* cite Ps 69:21 only implicitly. But the Synoptics diminish even that resonance by splitting the twin elements of gall and vinegar into two units. In Mark 15:22 Jesus is offered "wine mingled with myrrh" which Matt 27:33 changes to "wine mingled with gall." Then in Mark 15:36 (=Matt 27:48 = Luke 23:36), "one ran and, filling a sponge full of vinegar, put it on a reed and gave it to him to drink." While the biblical resonances may still be discerned in the Synoptics, they have certainly not improved on *Gos. Pet.* 5:16 where the conjunction of gall and vinegar makes the allusion much more secure.

Gos. Pet. 5:16–17 reads, "And one of them said, 'Give him to drink gall with vinegar.' And they mixed it and gave him to drink. And they fulfilled *all things* and *completed* the measure of their sins on their *head*." Now compare John 19:28–30, noting the italicized words, "After this Jesus, knowing that *all* was now finished, said (to fulfil the scripture), 'I thirst.' A bowl full of vinegar stood there; so they put a sponge full of the vinegar on hyssop and held it to his mouth. When Jesus had received the vinegar, he said, 'It is *finished*'; and he bowed his *head* and gave up his spirit." On the one hand, John has made the allusion to Ps 69:21 more explicit and, on the other, he has quarried *Gos. Pet.* 5:17 (all things, finished/completed, head) to create his own 19:30.

I consider that the gall and vinegar theme is much more original in *Peter* than in the twin scenes of Mark and Matthew or in the more explicitly biblical scene in John.

THE PASSION IN THE GOSPEL
OF PETER AND MARK

I mentioned already that Mark alone has no element common only to it and *Peter*. I focus therefore on a unit which is characteristically but not exclusively Markan.

The Final Confession appears outside the passion narrative in *Peter* but within it in Mark 15:39 = Matt 27:54 = Luke 23:47. In *Gos. Pet.* 11:45, that is, within *GP 4: Resurrection and Confession* (9:35–11:49), the following appears: "When those who were of the centurion's company saw this, they hastened by night to Pilate, abandoning the sepulchre which they were guarding, and reported everything that they had seen, being full of disquietude and saying, 'In truth he was the Son of God.'" Since they have just witnessed a transcendental epiphany, their reaction is no more than might be expected.

But this confession is linked by Mark 15:39 not to the moment of Jesus' resurrection but to the manner of Jesus' death, and now it is a confession of the centurion alone: "And when the centurion, who stood facing him, saw that he thus breathed his last, he said, '*Truly* this man *was* the *Son of God!*'" The italicized words are the same in the Greek of *Peter* and Mark.

On the one hand, that agrees completely with Markan christology. Throughout his gospel Mark uses injunctions to silence during exorcisms and healings to warn against misunderstanding their meaning. Such power cannot save Jesus from his suffering destiny. And Mark concludes with an empty tomb and an absent Jesus rather than a risen apparition and a present Jesus to emphasize that suffering and loss are also the lot of the followers of Jesus. At, and only at, the parousia, will Jesus' power be fully revealed (9:1). As Werner H. Kelber summarizes this theology, "In Mk 14–16 the Mkan passion Christology is accompanied by the shadow of its own negation. The Christology of the suffering Son of Man, King, and Son of God is

developed in contradiction to an opposite concept of Messiah-
ship, one of miraculous demonstration of power. At crucial
points in Mk 14–16 theme alternates with countertheme, claim
meets counterclaim, and confession is pitted against anti-con-
fession" (1976:165). The removal of the Final Confession from
the moment of miraculous resurrection to that of suffering
crucifixion is just such a countertheme.

On the other hand, look at how Luke 23:47 and Matt 27:54
handle this strange event in Mark 15:39. Luke mutes the incident by connecting it not just to Jesus' death as in Mark but
more vaguely to "what had taken place," and he renders the
confession more juridical than christological: "Now when the
centurion saw what had taken place, he praised God, and said,
'Certainly this man was innocent.'" Matthew reads more like a
full conflation of *Peter* and Mark, of *Peter's* intention within
Mark's location: "When the centurion and those who were with
him, keeping watch over Jesus, saw the earthquake and what
took place, they were filled with awe, and said, 'Truly, this was
the Son of God!'" Notice that Matthew has a plural confession,
as in *Peter*, and that they are "keeping watch over Jesus," just as
earlier in 27:36, phrases more suitable to guarding a tomb than
finishing a crucifixion.

I consider the most plausible understanding of those relations is that Mark knew and used *Peter*, and that Matthew
knew and used both *Peter* and Mark. Matt 27:54 is an almost
classic Matthean conflation of twin sources, of Mark 15:39 with
Gos. Pet. 11:45.

THE PASSION IN THE GOSPEL
OF PETER AND MATTHEW

There are two elements (Nos. 1, 17) found only in *Peter* and
Matthew: the Hand Washing in *Gos. Pet.* 1:1 and Matt 27:24a;
the Earthquake in *Gos. Pet.* 6:21 and Matt 27:51b. I shall concentrate on the second one.

141

The earthquake is very well integrated into the narrative sequence of *Peter*. It is specifically the earth's reaction to the deposition of Jesus in *Gos. Pet.* 6:21, "And then the Jews drew the nails from the hands of the Lord and laid him on the earth. And the whole earth shook and there came a great fear."

In Matt 27:51, however, the earthquake is one of the presumably eschatological phenomena at the death of Jesus which are recorded without apparently having any effect on anyone: "and behold, the curtain of the temple was torn in two, from top to bottom; and the earth shook, and the rocks were split."

I consider, therefore, that the earthquake is much more original in *Peter* than in Matthew.

THE PASSION IN THE GOSPEL OF PETER AND LUKE

There are two elements (Nos. 2, 9) found only in *Peter* and Luke: Herod's Role in *Gos. Pet.* 1:1, 2 and Luke 23:6–12; the Criminal Confesses in *Gos. Pet.* 4:13 and Luke 23:39–43. I shall concentrate on the second one.

After the crucifiers have divided the garments of Jesus, *Gos. Pet.* 4:13 says that, "one of the malefactors rebuked them, saying, 'We have landed in suffering for the deeds of wickedness which we have committed, but this man, who has become the saviour of men, what wrong has he done you?'" This incident of the good criminal appears as follows in Luke 23:39–43. "One of the criminals who were hanged railed at him, saying, 'Are you not the Christ? Save yourself and us!' But the other rebuked him saying, 'Do you not fear God, since you are under the same sentence of condemnation? And we indeed justly; for we are receiving the due reward of our deeds; but this man has done nothing wrong.' And he said, 'Jesus, remember me when you come into your kingdom.' And he said to him, 'Truly, I say to you, today you will be with me in Paradise.'"

One might be able to argue in this case for either *Peter's* contraction or Luke's expansion of the incident. Notice, for example, that John 19:18 leaves the character of the two other crucifieds unspecified while Mark 15:27 = Matt 27:38 describes them as "robbers" or insurgent rebels (*lēstai*). But *Gos. Pet.* 4:10, 13 identifies them as "malefactors" (*kakourgoi*) and so also does Luke 23:32, 33, 39 identify them as "criminals" (*kakourgoi*). Since this term is used only once more in the New Testament, at 2 Tim 2:9, that is a strong connection, but, of course it does not prove which way dependence lies. There is, however, one small feature that persuades me of Luke's dependence on *Peter* rather than the reverse. In *Peter* the good criminal accuses the crucifiers but in Luke he rebukes his companion criminal because of what he had said. And what he had said to Jesus was: "Are you not the *Christ? Save yourself* and us!" Those italicized words and the whole theme of mocking challenge derives from Mark 15:29–32 = Matt 27:39–43 = Luke 23:35. Note the "save yourself" in Mark 15:30 and the "Christ" in 15:32. In other words, this phrase is redactionally Lukan and is precisely what is absent from *Peter*.

I consider, therefore, that Luke 23:39–43 is dependent on *Gos. Pet.* 4:13 and that is why he has "criminals/malefactors" for this incident rather than Mark's "robbers." A reverse dependence is possible but much less likely.

THE PASSION IN THE GOSPEL OF PETER AND JOHN

There are two elements (Nos. 4, 10) found only in *Peter* and John: the Eve of Passover in *Gos. Pet.* 2:5b and John 19:14; the Legs Unbroken in *Gos. Pet.* 4:14 and John 19:31–37. I shall concentrate on the second one.

Immediately following the incident where the Criminal Confesses and indeed as its conclusion, *Gos. Pet.* 4:14 has, "And they were wroth with him and commanded that his legs should not be broken, so that he might die in torments." Although the he/his could refer to Jesus, the more obvious reading is that it is the good criminal's legs which are unbroken and that in punishment for his rebuke.

John 19:31–37, however, has this version. "Since it was the day of Preparation, in order to prevent the bodies from remaining on the cross on the sabbath (for that sabbath was a high day), the Jews asked Pilate that their legs might be broken, and that they might be taken away. So the soldiers came and broke the legs of the first, and of the other who had been crucified with him; but when they came to Jesus and saw that he was already dead, they did not break his legs. But one of the soldiers pierced his side with a spear, and at once there came out blood and water. He who saw it has borne witness—his witness is true, and he knows that he tells the truth—that you also may believe. For these things took place that the scripture might be fulfilled, 'Not a bone of him shall be broken.' And again another scripture says, 'They shall look on him whom they have pierced.'"

Behind the Legs Unbroken incident are such texts as Exod 12:46; Num 9:12; Ps 34:20 (33:21 in LXX). *Peter* applied it implicitly to the good criminal, John applies it explicitly to Jesus. I find it absolutely unbelievable that *Gos. Pet.* 4:14 is derived from John 19:31–37. I can easily imagine why John would have constructed that superb and explicit fulfilment by transferring the Legs Unbroken element from the good criminal to Jesus but I cannot imagine what *Peter* would have been doing in destroying that fulfilment and transferring the act in the opposite direction. As P. Gardner-Smith put it long ago, "if we seek a proof that 'Peter' did not know John surely we have it here" (1925–26a:256).

I consider, therefore, that the dependence here is of John on *Peter* and not the other way around.

THE PASSION IN TRADITION

Transmission

In the preceding analyses I looked only at certain key parallels between *Peter* and the four intracanonical gospels: Gall and Vinegar, Final Confession, Deposition and Quake, Criminal Confesses, Legs Unbroken. My conclusion is that *Peter* is not dependent on them but rather that all four of them are dependent on *Peter*, at least for their passion narrative. That is to say, *GP 1: Crucifixion and Deposition* is the source of Mark 15:15b–39 = Matt 27:24–54 = Luke 23:6–48 = John 19:16–37. It is this single unified source which is the primary reason for the remarkably homogeneous passion narrative in all four intracanonical gospels.

At this point I go beyond the evidence just presented and offer a working hypothesis or challenge for reasearch. *Is there any compelling evidence for another passion source anywhere in the four intracanonical gospels or can they all be adequately and plausibly explained as layers of redactional expansion on that single primary source?*

My own working hypothesis is this. (1) The first stage of the passion narrative was *GP 1: Crucifixion and Deposition* (1:1–6:22, but without 2:3–5a). (2) The second stage was Mark's redaction of that source, omitting, developing, and creating units in terms of his own quite different and distinctive theology. I see no compelling evidence that Mark's passion narrative includes anything more than a profound redaction of *Peter*. (3) The third stage was that of Matthew and Luke, each of whom had available the only two earlier passion narratives, that of *Peter* and of Mark. Their own redactions consisted of replacing within the Markan narrative certain elements from *Peter* that Mark had deliberately omitted, for example, the Hand Washing and Earthquake by Matthew, and Herod's Role and the Criminal Confesses by Luke. Once again, I see no compelling reason to postulate other sources for them than *Peter*, Mark, and their own authorial creativity. (4) The fourth stage is the most complicated and tentative. But again, and as a working hypothesis, John seems to have had only *Peter* and the Synoptics as sources for his own passion narrative. His own most creative and theological composition from those sources also involved replacing certain elements omitted from *Peter* by Mark, for example, the Eve of Passover crucifixion and the Legs Unbroken incident.

If that hypothesis can be sustained, it means, to repeat myself, that *GP 1: Crucifixion and Deposition* is the only source for Mark 15:15b–39, that those two together are the only sources for Matt 27:24–54, Luke 23:6–48, and that those earlier ones are the only sources for John 19:16–37. This is what explains the passion narratives' basic agreement in sequence and striking correspondence in content.

Intertextuality

I suggested in Case Study 2 that Old Testament texts such as Ps 118:22–23 and Isa 5:1–7 had hermeneutically infiltrated the parable of *The Evil Tenants* and helped form the very text of its transmission. In Case Study 3 a special feature of such infiltration was mentioned. There the quotation from Isa 29:13 first appeared in *The Question about Tribute* in Eger P 2, fragment 2r, lines 54–59. Thence it was moved by Mark to become part of *The Question about Purity* in Mark 7:6–7. Old Testament texts and biblical prophecies both infiltrate and then migrate along the strands of the Jesus tradition. Those cases had to do with the words of Jesus' teachings. Case Study 5 makes it clear that exactly the same processes took place and indeed took place even more profoundly, in the *events* of Jesus' life.

I think it is much easier to accept this conclusion for the words than for the events. What could be more magnificently realistic than the passion narrative which we have known so well and so long in stained glass and story, in art and music and drama? But what ruled the creation of the passion narrative: was it historical recall or biblical prophecy? For example, we are repeatedly told that Jesus was silent during the passion: at the crucifixion in *Gos. Pet.* 4:10b, before the Sanhedrin in Mark 14:61 = Matt 26:63, before Herod in Luke 23:9, and before Pilate in Mark 15:5 = Matt 27:14. Is all or any of this historical memory or is it fulfilment of Isa 53:7, "He was oppressed, and he was afflicted, yet he opened not his mouth; like a lamb that is led to the slaughter, and like a sheep that before its shearers is dumb, so he opened not his mouth"?

Helmut Koester points out what is often the deep and controlling structure of our surface decisions on such individual items

> The judgment about the passion narrative of the *Gospel of Peter* and its relationship to the canonical gospels depends upon one's general view of the development of the passion narrative. If one assumes that there was once an older historical report which was later supplemented with materials drawn from scriptural prophecy, the *Gospel of Peter* with its rich references and allusions to such scriptural passages will appear as secondary and derivative. There are, however, serious objections to this hypothesis. Form, structure, and life situation of such a historical passion report and its transmission have never been clarified. The alternative is more convincing: In the beginning there was only the belief that Jesus' suffering, death, and burial, as well as his resurrection, happened "according to the Scriptures" (1 Cor 15:3–4). The very first narratives about Jesus' suffering and death would not have made the attempt to remember what actually happened. Rather, they would have found both the rationale and content of Jesus' suffering and death in the memory of those passages in the Psalms and Prophets which spoke about the suffering of the righteous (1980:127).

In the final analysis, therefore, whether one accepts or rejects the thesis offered in Case Study 5 may not depend on the cogency of the individual arguments but on whether one can accept such radical intertextuality in which biblical prophecy dictates the very details of what otherwise reads like an historical account. My own proposal is that we are probably incapable at this late stage of ever realizing how absolutely little the followers of Jesus knew about the details of the passion and crucifixion. But even if there had been present a neutral historian, would his account have been actually more correct? In the light of the subsequent history of Christianity and the Roman Empire, were not they more correct who said that the sun darkened, the earth shook, and the heavens opened?

10   CASE STUDY 6
BURIAL AND TOMB

The preceding case involved only one unit, *GP 1: Crucifixion and Deposition,* and its intracanonical parallels. This case includes three units. My proposal is that (1) *GP 3: Tomb and Guards* (7:25–9:34) was part of the original Passion-Resurrection Source, that (2) the redactor added to this both *GP 2: Joseph and Burial* (6:23–24) before it, and *GP 5: Women and Youth* (12:50-13:57) after it, and that (3) these new and later units from the intracanonical gospels were carefully integrated into the earlier ones.

BURIAL AND GUARDS
IN THE GOSPEL OF PETER

I mentioned in the last section that the Hand Washing and Earthquake elements were found only in *Gos. Pet.* 1:1 and 6:21, Matt 27:24a and 27:51b respectively. The presence of guards at the tomb of Jesus is another but even more major theme found only in *Peter* and Matthew. At the moment I consider only the *Tomb and Guards* in *Gos. Pet.* 7:25–9:34 and Matt 27:62–66. Other segments of this theme will be discussed later. The parallel elements in the *Tomb and Guards* unit are given in Figure 6.

I consider that the *Tomb and Guards* unit was original to *Peter,* was omitted by Mark, but was reinserted into his Markan source by Matthew. In studying it, I shall concentrate on its first element, the Motive and Request, since that is where dependence questions can most easily be decided.

There are two different reasons for the request for guards at the tomb: the people's repentance in *Peter* but Jesus' prophecy in Matthew.

149

Figure 6

Literary Elements	Peter	Matthew
1 Motive and Request	7:25; 8:28–30	27:62–64
2 Response of Pilate	8:31a	27:65
3 Stone Sealed	8:31b-33a	27:66a
4 Guards Set	8:33b	27:66b
5 Crowds Visit Tomb	9:34	

People's Repentance and the Guards. The causal connections between the three sections of the original Passion-Resurrection Source were very well constructed. Of present concern is that between *GP 1: Crucifixion and Deposition* and its immediately following *GP 3: Tomb and Guards.*

Instead of the somewhat laconic statement that there was darkness from noon to three, as in Matt 27:45=Mark 15:33= Luke 23:44, the *Gospel of Peter* tells how the darkness started (5:15), affected people (5:18), included the rent veil (5:20) and the earthquake (6:21b), and then ended (6:22). This is an important and necessary preparation for the repentance of the people in 7:25, "Then the Jews and the elders and the priests, perceiving what great evil they had done to themselves, began to lament and to say, 'Woe on our sins, the judgment and the end of Jerusalem is drawn nigh.'" And it is this repentance which leads directly to the guards at the tomb in 8:28–30, "But the Scribes and Pharisees and elders, being assembled together and hearing that all the people were murmuring and beating their breasts, saying, 'If at his death these exceeding great signs have come to pass, behold how righteous he was!'—were afraid and came to Pilate, entreating him and saying, 'Give us soldiers that we may watch his sepulchre for three days, lest his disciples come and steal him away and the people suppose that he is risen from the dead, and do us harm.'" Thus *GP 1: Crucifixion and Deposition* gives careful preparation for *GP 3: Tomb and Guards.* The miracles at the death of Jesus lead to the repentance of the people and this leads in turn to the fear of the authorities and hence to the guards at the tomb.

A footnote. The repentance of the people in *Gos. Pet.* 7:25 and 8:28 has a parallel only in Luke 23:48, "and all the multitudes who assembled to see the sight, when they saw what had taken place, returned home beating their breasts." This second unit from the original Passion-Resurrection Source, *GP 2: Tomb and Guards*, has, therefore, a significant parallel not only with the guards in Matthew but also with this repentance in Luke. I consider, however, that Luke depends for this theme on *Peter* and not the reverse. The common "beating their breasts" in *Gos. Pet.* 8:28 and Luke 23:48 is an integral and causal component of the ongoing narrative in that former text but only a passing comment in the latter one.

Jesus' Prophecy and the Guards. In Matthew, of course, there has been no such repentance: see Matt 27:25! Thus in 27:63–64 there has to be a different motivation for the request. It is this: "'Sir, we remember how that imposter said, whilst he was still alive, "After three days I will rise again." Therefore order the tomb to be made secure until the third day, lest his disciples go and steal him away, and tell the people, "he has risen from the dead," and the last fraud will be worse than the first.'" The key change is Jesus' earlier prophecy of his resurrection rather than the people's earlier signs of repentance and fear.

Another footnote. *Peter* has obviously emphasized the security and publicity of the tomb. It is closed, sealed, and protected by both Roman and Jewish authorities (8:31–33) and, besides that, "early in the morning, when the sabbath dawned, there came a crowd from Jerusalem and the country round about to see the sepulchre that had been sealed" (9:34). This is quite uniquely *Peter*. But there is one vestige of it in Matthew. He locates the request to Pilate on the "next day" after the crucifixion. This is not very wise, since the tomb was then unguarded one whole night. I suggest he took the chronological note from *Peter* who locates the arival of the crowds, but not of course of the guards, on that next, or Sabbath day.

It is clear that *GP 3: Tomb and Guards* is already heavily freighted with apologetic and polemical overtones in *Peter* but the account in Matt 27:62–66 is more likely dependent on it rather than the reverse. This is most obvious in the Motive and Request element. I see no compelling reason to postulate either independent tradition in Matthew or even a common source behind *Peter* and Matthew. The self-consistent, self-coherent, and self-contained unity of the Passion-Resurrection Source quite adequately explains Matt 27:62–66 as well as those preparatory hints about the watching guards in Matt 27:36, 54.

BURIAL AND JOSEPH
IN THE GOSPEL OF PETER

My proposal is that *GP 2: Joseph and Burial* (6:23–24) was inserted between the original closed sequence of *GP 1: Crucifixion and Deposition* (1:1–6:22) and *GP 3: Tomb and Guards* (7:25–9:34). The insertion was prepared for by the preliminary inclusion of Joseph's request at *Gos. Pet.* 2:3–5a. This is the first of the three redactional preparations mentioned earlier.

The incident concerning *Joseph and Burial* is in all five gospels. Its parallel elements are given in Figure 7.

Figure 7

Literary Elements	*Peter*	Matthew	Mark	Luke	John
1 Motive and Request	2:5		15:42		19:31,42
	6:23b	27:57–58a	15:43	23:50–52	19:38a
2 Response of Pilate		27:58b	15:44–45		19:38b
3 Spices & Nicodemus					19:39–40
4 Burial by Joseph	6:24	27:59–60	15:46-47	23:53	19:41

Once again, I concentrate on the Motive and Request element which is probably the most important one in deciding the question of source and dependence.

As indicated in the above table, there are actually two separate motivations for the request and the burial. The first one was respect for Law, and applied even to Jesus' enemies; the second one was respect for Jesus, and applied only to his friends.

First Motive: Respect for Law. This first motivation for Jesus' burial was already given within the Passion-Resurrection Source at *Gos. Pet.* 5:15, "Now it was midday and a darkness covered all Judaea. And they became anxious and uneasy lest the sun had already set, since he was still alive. <For> it stands written for them: the sun should not set on one that has been put to death." The idea is already implicitly present here that the Jewish authorities would have wanted Jesus buried by evening out of respect for the Law, and, if no one else did it, they would have presumably done it themselves.

The legal text in question here is Deut 21:22–23, "And if a man has committed a crime punishable by death and he is put to death, and you hang him on a tree, his body shall not remain all night upon the tree, but you shall bury him the same day, for a hanged man is accursed by God; you shall not defile your land which the Lord your God gives you for an inheritance."

There is also another text with an application of this law, which is even more important for the situation of Jesus. Joshua 10 concerns the defeat of the five kings of southern Canaan on the day when the sun stood still at Gibeon. In Josh 10:17–18, "it was told to Joshua, 'The five kings have been found, hidden in the cave at Mekkedah.' And Joshua said, 'Roll great stones against the mouth of the cave and set men by it to guard them.'" Later on, in 10:26–27, Joshua "smote them and put them to death, and he hung them on five trees. And they hung upon the trees until evening; but at the time of the going down of the sun, Joshua commanded, and they took them down from the trees, and threw them into the cave where they had hidden themsleves, and they set great stones against the mouth of the cave, which remain to this very day."

I consider that Deut 21:22–23 lies behind the concern of the Jewish authorities in *Gos. Pet.* 5:15. But, even more significantly, I consider that Deuteronomy 21 led to Joshua 10, so that the buried body, great rolled stone, and posted guards of that latter text gave all the basic details for *GP 3: Tomb and Guards.*

This also clarifies the content of the redactional preparation for the insertion of *GP 2: Joseph and Burial* at *Gos. Pet.* 2:3–5a. This reads, "Now there stood there Joseph, the friend of Pilate and of the Lord, and knowing that they were about to crucify him he came to Pilate and begged the body of the Lord for burial. And Pilate sent to Herod and begged his body. And Herod said, 'Brother Pilate, even if no one had begged him, we should bury him, since the Sabbath is drawing on. For it stands written in the law: the sun should not set on one that has been put to death." This little compositional gem effects a double mediation between the earlier *GP 1: Crucifixion and Deposition,* and the later *GP 2: Joseph and Burial.* First, it mediates between control of the crucifixion by Herod, as in *GP 1*, and control of the crucifixion by Pilate, as in *GP 2.* Joseph is Pilate's friend, so he must approach him. But Herod is in charge, so Pilate must approach Herod. Second, their interchange serves another mediation. Herod's comment to Pilate combines both the burial by evening, as in *GP 1*, and the mention of the oncoming Sabbath, as in *GP 2*, from Mark 15:42=John 19:31.

The trajectory of this first motive, respect for the Law, is primarily a declining one. (a) It is a problem for Jesus' enemies in *Gos. Pet.* 5:15, and it is a general imperative based on Deut 21:22–23 and Jos 10:26–27. It has nothing specifically to do with Sabbath or Passover although, of course, such days might render the general imperative more compelling. (b) It is still a problem for Jesus' enemies in John 19:31, "Since it was the day of Preparation, in order to prevent the bodies from remaining on the cross on the sabbath (for that sabbath was a high day), the Jews asked Pilate that their legs might be broken, and that they might be taken away." But the problem becomes one for Jesus' friends by John 19:42, "So because of the Jewish day of Preparation, as the tomb was close at hand, they laid Jesus there." Now, however, the problem is that it is the eve of both Sabbath and Passover. Still, John 19:31–42 wants to keep both traditions on this point, as best he can. (c) By Mark 15:42 this is becoming residual "And when evening had come, since it was the day of Preparation, that is, the day before the sabbath, Joseph . . . went to Pilate." There is now nothing about Jesus' enemies or the general imperative, only the Sabbath and Joseph. (d) It is even more residual in Matt 27:57, "when it was evening . . . Joseph . . . went to Pilate." (e) Luke 23:54–56 redeems the situation by changing the whole point of the incident: "It was the day of Preparation, and the sabbath was beginning. The women who had come with him from Galilee followed, and saw the tomb, and how his body was laid; then they returned, and prepared spices and ointments. On the sabbath they rested according to the commandment." Oncoming evening and legal obedience are taken away from the inimical authorities seeking to bury Jesus swiftly, as in *Peter*, and transferred to the faithful women unable to anoint Jesus adequately, as in Luke. And this, of course, prepares well for Luke 24:1, "But on the first day of the week, at early dawn, they went to the tomb, taking the spices which they had prepared."

The first motive, therefore, is slowly but steadily disappearing from the tradition, although John manages to reinstate it somewhat, but for his own purposes. Jewish respect for Jewish Law is not a growing concern of the tradition's trajectory.

Second Motive: Respect for Jesus. How exactly does one get from a burial by Jesus' enemies to a burial by Jesus' friends? One needs, obviously, a somewhat in-between character, somebody with a double or ambiguous allegiance. And that is exactly what Joseph of Arimathea turns out to be.

Mark 15:43 describes him with twin qualities as, "Joseph of

Arimathea, a respected member of the council, who was also himself looking for the kingdom of God." This connects him, on the one hand, to the authorities who oversaw the burial in *Peter*, but, on the other, it begins the process of taking the burial away from Jesus' enemies and giving it to his friends and followers. There is, however, an obvious problem with this in-between position, with this Christian Sanhedrist. Where, one might wonder, was he when Jesus needed him most? Matthew, Luke, and John sense this narrative problem quite clearly and solve it quite resolutely. Matt 27:57 changes the Sanhedrist part and instead says "there came a rich man from Arimathea, named Joseph, who was also a disciple of Jesus." Luke 23:50–51 glosses the Sanhedrist with almost agonizing care, "Now there was a man named Joseph from the Jewish town of Arimathea. He was a member of the council, a good and righteous man, who had not consented to their purpose and deed, and he was looking for the kingdom of God." John 19:38 omits the Sanhedrist part completely, and has, "Joseph of Arimathea, who was a disciple of Jesus, but secretly, for fear of the Jews."

I find no compelling reason to postulate any tradition about Joseph of Arimathea except that in Mark and derived from him. It was Mark who began the process of taking Jesus' burial away from his enemies and giving it to his friends and he did so by using the in-between character, Joseph of Arimathea. In deference to the Passion-Resurrection Source Mark still kept him in the Sanhedrin and was deliberately vague about his Christian credentials, he was "looking for the kingdom of God." Thereafter, of course, it would be necessary either to redeem him within the Sanhedrin, as in Luke, or to remove him completely from the Sanhedrin, and make him a full disciple of Jesus, as in Matthew and John.

The trajectory of this second motive, respect for Jesus, is as clearly an ascending one as the trajectory of that first motive, repect for Law, was a descending one. (a) In Mark 15:46 there is a "linen shroud" and "a tomb which had been hewn out of the rock." (b) In Luke 23:53 there is a "linen shroud" and "a rock-hewn tomb, where no one had ever yet been laid." (c) In Matt 27:59-60 it is a "clean linen shroud" and Joseph's "own new tomb, which he had hewn in the rock." (d) Finally, there is John 19:39-40. He introduces Nicodemus, known to us from 3:1 and 7:50, and instead of a hurried and somewhat inadequate burial necessitating later and fuller anointing, as in Mark 15:47; 16:1 and Luke 23:55-56; 24:1, there is now a full and even regal embalming. "Nicodemus also, who had at first come to him by night, came bringing a mixture of myrrh and aloes, about a hundred pounds' weight. They took the body of Jesus, and bound it in linen cloths with the spices, as is the burial custom of the Jews. Now in the place where he was crucified there was a garden, and in the garden a new tomb where no one had ever been laid . . . they laid Jesus there."

If the tradition of the first motive, respect for the Law must decrease, that of the second motive, respect for Jesus, must increase.

BURIAL AND WOMEN
IN THE GOSPEL OF PETER

My proposal is that *GP 5: Women and Youth* (12:50-13:57) was added at the end of the originally closed sequence of the Passion-Resurrection Source in *GP 1-3-4*. The addition was prepared for by the preliminary mentions of the "youth" (*neaniskos*) in *Gos. Pet.* 9:37 and 11:43-44. This is the second of the three redactional preparations mentioned earlier. The *Women and Youth* incident is found in all five gospels. Its parallel elements are given in Figure 8.

In this instance my primary proof that *Peter* is dependent here on the intracanonical gospels, that is, essentially on Mark, derives from his redactional preparation itself but especially since this preparatory insert involves the "youth" in the tomb, an item which is quintessentially Markan.

157

Figure 8

Literary Elements	Peter	Matthew	Mark	Luke	John
1 Motivation	12:50–51	28:1	16:1–2	24:1	(20:1)
2 Discussion	12:52–54		16:3		
3 Stone Removed	13:55a	28:2	16:4	24:2	20:2
4 Apparition	13:55b	28:3–4	16:5	24:3–5a	20:14
5 Address	13:56	28:5–6	16:6	24:5b–8	20:15–16
6 Command		28:7	16:7		20:17
7 Result	13:57	28:8	16:8	24:9–11	20:18

The Redactional Preparation

There are two steps in the preparatory insertion. First, in 9:36, "two men come down" from heaven to the tomb of Jesus. In 9:37, "both the young men (*neaniskoi*) entered in" the tomb. Then in 10:39, "three men come out from the sepulchre, and two of them sustaining the other [Jesus]." Within three successive verses, an equation of "men" and "young men" has been quietly established. Second, in 11:43–45, immediately after the guards have seen the resurrection of Jesus, this follows: "Those men therefore took counsel with one another to go and report this to Pilate. And whilst they were still deliberating, the heavens were again seen to open, and a man descended and entered the sepulchre. When those who were of the centurion's company saw this, they hastened by night to Pilate. . . . " Notice how you can read the narrative quite sequentially from 10:42 (resurrection) straight into 11:45 (report) and omit the inserted 11:43 (deliberation) which introduces 11:44 (man from heaven). But, of course, when later the story turns to the *Women and Youth* addition, all is prepared for them to find in the tomb "a young man (*neaniskos*)" in 13:55. In summary:

(i) "men" (9:36) = "young men" (9:37) = "men" (10:39);

(ii) "man" (11:44) = "young man" (13:55).

It is hard to imagine anything more deliberate or obvious than this. But it indicates how carefully the redactor wished to integrate the later and dependent *GP 5* (young man) with the earlier and independent *GP 4* (men).

Discussion and Command

Of the seven elements in *GP 5: Women and Youth* these two require special comment.

Discussion. The Motivation and Discussion elements in *Gos. Pet.* 12:50–54 reads as follows. "Early in the morning of the Lord's day Mary Magdalene, a woman disciple of the Lord—for fear of the Jews, since (they) were inflamed with wrath, she had not done at the sepulchre of the Lord what women are wont to do for those beloved of them who die—took with her women friends and came to the sepulchre where he was laid. And they feared lest the Jews should see them, and said, 'Although we could not weep and lament on that day when he was crucified, yet let us now do so at his sepulchre. But who will roll away for us the stone also that is set on the entrance to the sepulchre, that we may go in and sit beside him and do what is due?—For the stone was great,—and we fear lest any one see us. And if we cannot do so, let us at least put down at the entrance what we bring for a memorial of him and let us weep and lament until we have again gone home.'"

I read that rather tortured Discussion as a reflection of the difficulty the redactor has in announcing the discovery of an empty tomb to readers who have just seen it emptied. He has other narrative problems as well. He must explain to us who Mary Magdalene is, since there has been no preliminary mention of her in *Peter*, as there is, for example, in Mark 15:40,47. And then, having explained who she is and what she is about, he must explain why she did not do it earlier. To effect this, the Discussion is built up with three interwoven motifs: (a) "fear," mentioned thrice in 12:50, 52, 54 to explain why they had not done anything earlier, and borrowed from John 20:19; (b) "weep and lament," mentioned twice in 12:52, 54, and borrowed from John 20:11, 13, 15; (c) "anointing," mentioned thrice, but only indirectly and obliquely as "wont to do . . . what is due . . . what we bring" in 12:50, 53, 54, and borrowed from Mark 16:1= Luke 24:1. I presume that those indirect references to the anointing represent some embarrassment with the whole idea. But none of this is independent tradition. It is the redactor doing his best with a difficult narrative problem, namely, the addition of *GP 5: Women and Youth* after *GP 4: Resurrection and Confession* was already present.

Command. It has been suggested that at least Mark 16:7 is redactionally Markan within the pre-Markan complex of Mark 16:1–8. This might then indicate independent tradition in *Peter* since he completely lacks this particular element (Johnson: 15–17). I am not at all convinced by this argument. First, as I shall suggest later, I think that *all* of 16:1–8 is Markan redaction, that it was Mark himself who first created the *Women and Youth* incident. Second, and even if one does not concede that first point, Mark 16:7 is strange enough in itself for Matt 28:7 to rephrase it slightly in Matt 28:10, for Luke to rephrase it even more in 24:6–8, and for John 20:17 to rephrase it completely. There is quite enough reason for *Peter* not to touch it, especially since his Jesus, who will presumably be apearing to the disciples in the final fragmentary incident in *GP 6: Disciples and(?) Apparition* will be coming from heaven to earth and not just from Jerusalem to Galilee.

BURIAL AND TOMB IN TRADITION
Transmission

The schematic outline of the major stages in this tradition's transmission is given in Figure 9. For clarity's sake, I give them as separate strands, although, of course, they interweave together.

The Burial Tradition. There are three major stages. (a) In the original Passion-Resurrection Source it was taken for granted that Jesus' burial was completely under the motivation and control of his enemies: see *Gos. Pet.* 2:5, 5:15, 6:21. (b) In Mark 15:42–46 Jesus is buried by Joseph, mediating between enemies and friends, but in a necessarily hurried manner, hence Mark 15:47 and 16:1. I consider this to be a Markan creation. (c) John, who also reflects both those earlier stages in 19:31–37 and 19:38 respectively, gives the final stage with a magnificent embalming through Nicodemus in 19:40–42. The guiding thrust of this entire trajectory is to take Jesus' burial away from his enemies and give it to his friends and followers.

Figure 9

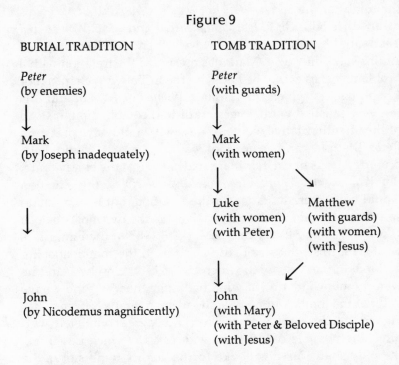

BURIAL TRADITION

Peter
(by enemies)

↓

Mark
(by Joseph inadequately)

↓

John
(by Nicodemus magnificently)

TOMB TRADITION

Peter
(with guards)

↓

Mark
(with women)

↓　＼

Luke   Matthew
(with women)   (with guards)
(with Peter)   (with women)
                        (with Jesus)

↓　　↙

John
(with Mary)
(with Peter & Beloved Disciple)
(with Jesus)

The Tomb Tradition. There are four major stages in this transmission. (a) In the original Passion-Resurrection Source there were only guards at the tomb but these were very well integrated into the narrative sequence: the miracles and repentance of *GP 1* led to the guards in *GP 3* and this to the witness and confession in *GP 4*. The guards were restored to his Markan source by Matt 27:62–66; 28:4, 11–15. (b) Mark has nothing about any guards but creates instead the empty tomb tradition of 16:1–8. I suggested this in 1976 arguing that there were no versions of this empty tomb tradition before Mark, that all our present versions derived from him, and that it was completely consistent with Markan redactional theology (135). I am even more convinced of this position now since the "youth in the tomb" of Mark 16:1–8 was derived by him from the "youth in the tomb" of the *Secret Gospel of Mark* in *MSLC* 2r:3, 4, 6. This means that both *GP 2: Joseph and Burial* and *GP 5: Women and Youth* are Markan creations and were thence derived by *Peter*. At this stage, however, Mark has presented the tradition with a problem, just as earlier he had with the in-between character of Joseph. He has given the tradition *Women and Youth* and it is not very satisfied with either part of that combination. Instead of the unauthoritative woman/women it would have preferred Peter/Disciples and instead of youth/angels it would have preferred Jesus himself. If Mark had created at the empty tomb, not *Women and Youth* but *Jesus and Disciples,* the situation would have been far easier for the tradition. But he did not do so and the tradition proceeds to solve it in the two most obvious ways. (c1) Luke 24:1–11 retells Mark 16:1–8 but then improves on it with this: "But Peter rose and ran to the tomb; stooping and looking in, he saw the linen cloths by themselves, and he went home wondering at what had happened." We now have Peter at the tomb, and not just the women. Frans Neirynck has argued that this is a Lukan creation and I agree completely with him: "the possible connections with Mk 16 (which is, I think, the only source used by Luke for his empty tomb story), the characteristically Lukan traits and the function of v. 12 in the composition of chapter 24 are, in my view, the indications for the Lukan origin of this little story" (175). (c2) Matt 28:9–10 adopts the alternative strategy. Instead of bringing Peter/

Disciples as well as the women to the tomb, he brings Jesus as well as the angel to the tomb: "And behold, Jesus met them and said, 'Hail!' And they came up and took hold of his feet and worshiped him. Then Jesus said to them, 'Do not be afraid; go and tell my brethren to go to Galilee, and there they will see me.'" This is based directly on the earlier dialogue between angel and women in Matt 28:5–7, derived itself from Mark 16:6–7. Once again, I agree with Frans Neirynck that this is a Matthean creation: "Matt. xxviii.1–10 presupposes no other gospel tradition than Mark xvi.1–8, and the christophany to the women (*vv.* 9–10) is best explained from the angelic message in Mark xvi.6–7 (1982b:295). (d) Finally, and once again, John manages to reflect all the previous developments of the tradition:

    (i) women at the tomb in 20:1,11–13;

    (ii) Peter at the tomb in 20:2–10;

    (iii) Jesus at the tomb in 20:14–18.

For women at the tomb, he has only Mary Magdalene in 20:1, but note the plural "we" in her report at 20:2. For Peter at the tomb, he has an exquisite counterpoint in 20:2–10. The Beloved Disciple runs, looks, and believes before Peter, but Peter is allowed to enter the tomb first. And for Jesus at the tomb, there is the interchange and new Command element in 20:14–18. Some scholars have seen independent and even very early tradition in all this. I find myself unable to accept this interpretation. John 20:1–18 is most easily and economically explained as a Johannine composition based on three different Synoptic ingredients: the women at the tomb from Mark 16:1–8, Peter at the tomb in Luke 24:12, and Jesus at the tomb in Matt 28:9–10. That dependence is hilariously evident in 20:2–10 where John bows to Luke 24:12 by letting Peter enter the tomb first but demolishes this precedence beforehand by having the Beloved Disciple get there and look in first and demolishes it afterwards by having only the Beloved Disciple come to faith from the experience. But dependence is plausibly possible for all of John

20:1–18. As Frans Neirynck concludes: "In 'a scenario in which John knew of the Synoptics' (D. M. Smith) one can imagine that 'he tried to make one consistent narrative' by relying on Luke in the first part (20.1–10) and on Matthew in the second part (20.11–18). This gives a plausible explanation for the duplication of Mary's announcement to the disciples in vv. 2 and 18 . . . The Synoptic influence . . . may have been determinative for the whole of the composition of Jn. 20.1–18" (1984:179).

Intertextuality

The preceding transmissional analysis concluded that the origins of the Burial and Tomb tradition were to be found in the Passion-Resurrection Source of *Peter*. But both parts of that tradition are themselves based on and derived from Old Testament texts.

The Burial tradition in the Passion-Resurrection Source stems from Deut 21:22–23. It is because of respect for this law that the tradition presumed the Jewish authorities would have buried Jesus themselves. Since they were in total charge of the crucifixion, they were in total control of the burial as well.

So also with the Tomb tradition in the Passion-Resurrection Source. The motifs of the tomb closed with a great rolled stone and of the guards posted to watch are derived from Josh 10:18, 26–27 which was an obvious step once Deut 21:22–23 drew attention to Josh 10:27.

Just as intertextuality created the narrative details of the Passion story, so also did it create those of the Burial and Tomb traditions.

11   CASE STUDY 7
RESURRECTION AND CONFESSION

This case involves two units. The more important one is *GP 4: Resurrection and Confession* (9:35–11:49) since the other one, *GP 6: Disciples and (?) Apparition* (14:58–60) is fragmentary. My proposal is that *GP 4* was originally the concluding unit of *GP 1-3-4* which constituted the Passion-Resurrection Source. The redactor of the *Gospel of Peter* intended, instead, to conclude with *GP 6*, which he was adapting from John 21:1–8, and for whose later addition he had earlier prepared through the insertion of *Gos. Pet.* 7:26–27.

RESURRECTION IN GOS. PET. 9:35–11:49

This is composed of three sections: (1) Jesus and the Two Men, in 9:35–10:42; (2) Pilate and the Guards, in 11:45–49; and (3) in between them, the redactional preparation for the following *GP 5: Women and Youth*, in 11:43–44.

Jesus and the Two Men

I look first at this incident in *Gos. Pet.* 9:35–10:42; then at other possibly independent versions of it elsewhere; and finally at Mark's transposition of it into the Transfiguration at 9:2–8.

Jesus and the Two Men in Peter.   Here is the text in this version, but with the redactional change italicized:

> Now in the night in which the Lord's day dawned, when the soldiers, two by two in every watch, were keeping guard, there rang out a loud voice in heaven, and they saw the heavens opened and two men come down from there in a great brightness and draw nigh to the sepulchre. That stone which had been laid against the entrance

165

to the sepulchre started of itself to roll and give way to the side, and the sepulchre was opened, and both the *young* men entered in. When now those soldiers saw this, they awakened the centurion and the elders—for they also were there to assist at the watch. And whilst they were relating what they had seen, they saw again three men come out from the sepulchre, and two of them sustaining the other, and a cross following them, and the heads of the two reaching to heaven, but that of him who was led of them by the hand over-passing the heavens. And they heard a voice out of the heavens crying, "Thou hast preached to them that sleep," and from the cross there was heard the answer, "Yea."

Very little of this is reflected in the intracanonical resurrection traditions, but Matthew, who reinstates more of *Peter* in the Markan framework than either Luke or John, has two minor reminiscences from it. And Luke also has a small but very interesting allusion to it.

1) Matthew. First, in *Gos. Pet.* 9:36–37 there is a conjunction of the arrival from heaven and the opening of the tomb but no direct and explicit causality. In Matt 28:2 there is both conjunction and direct causality: "for an angel of the Lord descended from heaven and came and rolled back the stone, and sat upon it." Second, in *Gos. Pet.* 10:41–42 there is the belief that while he was in the tomb Jesus preached and saved the just who had died before his advent. This is also found, for example, in the short liturgical creed in 1 Pet 3:18–19, "For Christ also died for sins once for all, the righteous for the unrighteous, that he might bring us to God, being put to death in the flesh but made alive in the spirit; in which he went and preached to the spirits in prison," and again in 4:6, "for this is why the gospel was preached even to the dead, that though judged in the flesh like men, they might live in the spirit like God." Matthew wishes to use this tradition but he does so rather awkwardly. He puts the resurrection of the earlier dead among the miracles at the crucifixion and then has, of course, to delay it until after the resurrection of Jesus. This is how he has it both ways, in Matt 27:51–53: "And behold, the curtain of the

temple was torn in two, from top to bottom; and the earth shook, and the rocks were split; *the tombs also were opened*, and many bodies of the saints who had fallen asleep were raised, *and coming out of the tombs after the resurrection* they went into the holy city and appeared to many." I consider that both those Matthean units derive from the Passion-Resurrection Source.

2) Luke. Three times in his writings Luke has "two men" appear. At the Transfiguration, Mark 9:4 had only "Elijah and Moses," but Luke 9:30 added "two men . . . Moses and Elijah." In the empty tomb, Mark 16:5 had, of course, "a young man," but Luke 24:4 has "two men." And at the Ascension, in Acts 1:10, Luke has, "And while they were gazing into heaven as he went, behold, two men stood by them in white robes." I consider that Luke's "two men" at Transfiguration/Tomb/Ascension derive from the "two men" of the Passion-Resurrection Source.

Jesus and the Two Men Elsewhere. There are two other major places where this tradition of Jesus and the Two Men describes the resurrection-ascension.

1) *Testament of Hezekiah.* This was originally a separate document but is now included within the *Ascension of Isaiah*, a text "extant in an Ethiopic version, two recensions of the Latin version, in a Slavonic recension, and in Coptic and Greek fragments. There is also a related Greek legend. The most debated issue has been the question of unity" (Collins: 84). R. H. Charles describes it as follows:

> The *Ascension of Isaiah* is a composite work of very great interest. In its present form we cannot be sure that it existed earlier than the latter half of the second century of our era. Its various constituents, however, and of these there were three, circulated independently as early as the first century. These were the Martyrdom of Isaiah, the Vision of Isaiah, and the Testament of Hezekiah. The first of these was of Jewish origin, . . . the other two . . . were the work of Christian writers. . . . The long lost Testament of Hezekiah, which is, I think, to be identified with iii.13b to iv.18 of our present work, is

167

unquestionably of great value in the insight it gives us into the history of the Christian Church at the close of the first century (xi–xii).

In Charles' analysis, then, the *Ascension of Isaiah* is composed of three units redactionally integrated together by a single final editor (xl-xliii):

(a) *Martyrdom of Isaiah,* in 1:1, 2a, 6b–13a; 2:1–8, 10–3:12; 5:1b–14;

(b) *Testament of Hezekiah,* in 3:13b–4:18;

(c) *Vision of Isaiah,* in 6:1–11:40;

(d) Redactional Connections, in 1:2b–6a, 13b; 2:9; 3:13a; 4:1a; 4:19–5:1a, 15, 16; 11:41–43.

My present interest is with that second section, the *Testament of Hezekiah* now contained within the *Ascension of Isaiah* 3:13b–4:18 (*NTA:* 2.647–50).

The compositional date for the *Testament of Hezekiah* can only be argued on internal evidence. Charles claims that "this vision, or testament, was written between 88–100 A.D." (xliv). The earliest date is derived from the fact that "the latest pretender to the Neronic role came forward in 88 A.D." and in *Ascen. Isa.* 4:2–4 "it is manifest that the belief in Nero being still alive had already been abandoned" (lxix, lxx). The latest date comes from *Ascen. Isa.* 4:13 which points to a time when few who actually saw Christ are still alive: "Though somewhat vague, it is sufficiently definite to enable us to conclude that the author cannot have written later than 100 A.D." (31). This presumes, of course, that both 3:13b–31 and 4:1–18 form an original unity, since the dating comes from that latter section.

The section of the *Testament of Hezekiah* which contains the tradition of Jesus and the Two Men (Angels) is in *Ascen. Isa.* 3:13b–18 (*NTA:* 2.647–48):

Through him the coming forth of the Beloved from the seventh heaven had been revealed, and his transformation, namely, the likeness of a man, and the persecution which he was to suffer, and the tortures with which the children of Israel were to afflict him, and [the coming] of the twelve disciples [and the] instruction, [and that he should before the Sabbath be crucified on the tree] and that he was to be crucified together with criminals, and that he would be buried in a sepulchre, and that the twelve who were with him would be offended because of him, and the watch of the guards of the grave, and the descent of the angel of the church which is in the heavens, whom he will summon in the last days; and that the angel of the Holy Spirit and Michael, the chief of the holy angels, would open his grave on the third day, and that the Beloved, sitting on their shoulders, will come forth and send out his twelve disciples, and that they will teach to all the nations and every tongue the resurrection of the Beloved, and that those who believe on his cross will be saved, and in his ascension to the seventh heaven, whence he came.

In that complex the most important verses for my present purpose are:

(a) Guards at the Tomb (3:14b)
(b) Angel of the Church Descends (3:15)
(c) Angels Open the Tomb (3:16)
(d) Jesus and the Two Angels (3:17a)

(a) Guards at the Tomb (3:14b). As seen already, the theme of the guards was present only in *Peter* and Matthew.

(b) Angel of the Church Descends (3:15). I am not at all certain what this sentence means and the original editors are not very helpful. Charles translates with, "And the descent of the angel of the Christian Church, which is in the heavens, whom He will summon on the last days," but footnotes that, "the text may also be rendered 'who will summon'" (19). Grenfell and Hunt, who edited the Greek fragment of *Ascen. Isa.* 2:4–4:4, restore and translate the mutilated Greek (1900:11) with, "and *that* the descent of the angel of the church which is in heaven ... in the last days" (1900:16). They comment that "the Greek in this section diverges somewhat from the Ethiopic, and, owing to the lacunae, a complete restoration is impossible" (1900:21). My own guess is that the verse refers to the descent to the dead between crucifixion and resurrection, but it is uncertain whether the angel replaces or accompanies Jesus on this mission. My reason is that the final redactor found it necessary to say in 4:21, "Moreover the descent of the Beloved into the realm of the dead is recorded in the section where the Lord says 'Behold, my servant is prudent'" in Isa 52:13 (*NTA*: 2.650). It seems as if the redactor thought the descent to the dead had been missed somewhere in 3:15. Also, this theme of the descent among the righteous dead reappers frequently in the *Vision of Isaiah* (*NTA*: 2.651–63). *Ascen. Isa.* 9:16 says that "when he has made spoil of the angel of death, he will arise on the third day"; 10:8, 14 has God command Jesus, "'Go and descend through all the heavens; descend to the firmament and to that world, even to the angel in the realm of the dead; but to Hell thou shalt not go. . . . And afterwards thou wilt ascend from the angels of death to thy place'"; and 11:19–20 says that "after this the adversary envied him and roused the children of Israel against him, not knowing who he was, and they delivered him to the king and crucified him, and he descended to the angel (of the underworld). In Jerusalem indeed I saw how he was crucified on the tree, and how he was raised after three days and remained (still many) days." (By the way, is that king Pilate or Herod Antipas?). These texts indicate that Jesus descended to the place of the righteous dead but not, of course, to Hell, as the place of the unrighteous dead. Therefore, although *Ascen. Isa.* 3:15 is not very clear, I presume it refers to the descent among the dead of Jesus and/or the angel of judgment.

(c) Angels Open The Tomb (3:16). The "two men" of *Peter* are here two angels. The first angel is unnamed, unless the lacuna in the Greek had "Gabriel" (Grenfell & Hunt, 1900:11, 16, 21; Charles: 19). But he is called "the angel of the Holy Spirit" and this also appears in the *Vision of Isaiah*: at *Ascen. Isa.* 7:23, "And I rejoiced greatly that those who love the Most High and his Beloved will at their end ascend thither by the angel of the Holy Spirit," and also at 11:33, "I saw the angel of the Holy Spirit sitting on the left" of God in the seventh heaven. The other

170

angel is Michael, the chief of the holy angels. These open Jesus' tomb, unlike *Gos. Pet.* 9:37 but like Matt 28:2.

(d) Jesus and the Two Angels (3:17a). The most interesting change, however, is in the motif of *height*. In *Gos. Pet.* 10:40 this appeared as "the heads of the two reaching to heaven, but that of him who was led of them by the hand overpassing the heavens." But in *Ascen. Isa.* 3:17a Jesus is seated on their shoulders. However, although the motif of *height* is present in both texts, the motif of *light* is present only in *Gos. Pet.* 9:36, "in a great brightness," but not in the *Testament of Hezekiah.*

The two accounts in the *Gospel of Peter* and the *Testament of Hezekiah* have as common elements: the guards at the tomb, the descent among the righteous dead, the opening of the tomb, the resurrection with two helpers. Although the difference between a narrative sequence and a credal recitation make it difficult to compare the two texts, it seems most likely that they are independent of one another and represent variations on a common tradition.

2) Codex Bobiensis. This manuscript "of which only ninety-six pages survive (fairly large portions of Mark; smaller parts of Matthew), is said, according to creditable tradition, to have belonged to St. Columban, who died in 615 at the monastery he founded at Bobbio in northern Italy. It is the most important, as regards text, of all the Old Latin copies, being undoubtedly the oldest existing representative of the African type. Dated by Burkitt and Souter to the fourth century, it was thought by Hoogterp to be 'a direct copy of an archetype of the end of the third century', and Lowe considered it, on palaeographical grounds, to have been copied from a second-century papyrus" (Metzger, 1977:315).

One of the peculiarities of this manuscript is that there is a description of the resurrection of Jesus inserted after Mark 16:3. "At one or two places the text of the gloss does not appear to be sound, and various emendations have been proposed:

'Subito autem ad horam tertiam tenebrae diei factae sunt per totam orbem terrae, et descenderunt de caelis angeli et surgent [surgentes?, surgente eo? surgit?] *in claritate vivi Dei* [viri duo?+et?] *simul ascenderunt cum eo; et continuo lux facta est. Tunc illae accesserunt ad monimentum....* ("But suddenly at the third hour of the day there was darkness over the whole circle of the earth, and angels descended from the heavens, and as he [the Lord] was rising [reading *surgente eo*] in the glory of the living God, at the same time they ascended with him; and immediately it was light. Then the women went to the tomb.... ")'.

The emendation *viri duo*, which in the context appears to be unnecessary, has been proposed in view of the account in the Gospel of Peter of two men who, having descended from heaven in a great brightness, brought Jesus out of the tomb" (Metzger, 1971:121–22).

Even without the emendation of "viri duo" (two men), this is obviously the same tradition:

(a) *Gospel of Peter*: two men, light, height;
(b) *Testament of Hezekiah*: two angels, height;
(c) Codex Bobiensis: two angels, light.

There is no clear evidence of dependence in the case of Codex Bobiensis but it is so short a gloss that certainty is not possible. There may be, then, three separate witnesses to this theme of Jesus' resurrection aided and accompanied by two men/angels.

Jesus and the Two Men in Mark. The suggestion that the Transfiguration was originally a resurrection appearance is by no means new and it is probably as easy to argue for the position as against it. Even for those who hold this view: "the process by which this experience was read back into the ministry of Jesus as a transformation is obscure" (Carlston: 240). My own proposal is quite specific. I think that Mark knew the Passion-Resurrection Source; that he adopted and adapted the Passion section quite thoroughly; but that he deliberately and radically rephrased, relocated, and reinterpreted the Resurrection section. In other words, it was Mark himself who turned Resurrection into Transfiguration.

The reason for this relocation is profoundly rooted in Markan theology. As I suggested earlier, the time between resurrection and parousia is, for Mark, the period of suffering and absence. It is emphatically not the period of apparition, protection, and consolation. For Mark, the Transfiguration, following immediately on the threat and promise of the parousia in 8:38–9:1, is not a glimpse of the resurrection but of the parousia. In its Markan context, "the transfiguration emerges as a parousia epiphany" (Kelber, 1974:76).

There are four main elements from the original Resurrection story in *Gos. Pet.* 9:35–10:42 which Mark transferred to the Transfiguration story in 9:2–8. (1) Two Companions. The "two men" of *Gos. Pet.* 9:36–10:40 become "Elijah with Moses" in Mark 9:4. (2) Height. The "heads of the two reaching to heaven, but that of him who was led of them by the hand overpassing the heavens" from *Gos. Pet.* 10:40 becomes simply "led them up a high mountain" in Mark 9:2. (3) Light (see Robinson, 1982:7–17). The "great brightness" of *Gos. Pet.* 9:36 becomes "his garments became glistening, intensely white, as no fuller on earth could bleach them" in Mark 9:3. (4) Voice from Heaven. The "voice out of the heavens crying" in *Gos. Pet.* 10:41 becomes "a voice came out of the cloud" in Mark 9:7.

The other main elements in Mark 9:2–8, such as the special role of Peter, James, and John in 9:2, the misunderstanding of Peter in 9:5–6a, and the general fear in 9:6b, are all typical redactional themes in Mark. For Mark, Peter and the inner three do not understand that this vision is not of the resurrected Lord come to dwell among them, but of the returning Lord who will only appear in the future.

I do not think that those preceding parallels are very persuasive in themselves. Mark has so completely recast the Resurrection into the Transfiguration that it is very easy to dismiss the very idea of such a relocation and reinterpretation. I myself am primarily persuaded of it because, as I suggested earlier, he knew and transposed the Final Confession from the Resurrection unit in *Gos. Pet.* 11:45 to become the Centurion's Confession at the crucifixion in Mark 15:39. I therefore wonder what he did with the rest of the Resurrection story from *Peter*. Under those circumstances, I am predisposed to accept a relocation and reinterpretation of the entire Resurrection story from *Peter* as the Transfiguration or proleptic parousia revelation in Mark.

Finally, Luke's "two men" at his Transfiguration, Empty Tomb, and Ascension, as seen earlier, makes me wonder if he did not appreciate exactly what Mark had done.

Pilate and the Guards

The guards appear in two of the Passion-Resurrection Source's three units. These and their Matthean parallels are given in Figure 10.

Figure 10

Literary Elements	*Gospel of Peter*	Matthew
1 Request on Tomb	7:25 + 8:28–33 (in GP 3)	27:62–66
2 Reaction at Tomb	10:38 (in GP 4)	28:4
3 Report from Tomb	11:45–49 (in GP 4)	28:11–15

I have deliberately phrased those elements to omit the specific protagonists because they are strikingly different in *Peter* and Matthew.

Request on Tomb. This concerns the request that the tomb be sealed and guarded. In both *Peter* and Matthew it is made by the Jewish authorities to Pilate. This unit was already considered in Case Study 6 under *GP 3: Tomb and Burial.* I emphasize, however, one point from that earlier study. In *Peter* the tomb is sealed and guarded by both Roman and Jewish authorities. The former supply the martial forces but both are present on guard: "And Pilate gave them Petronius the centurion with soldiers to watch the sepulchre. And with them there came elders and scribes to the sepulchre. And all who were there, together with the centurion and the soldiers, rolled thither a great stone and laid it against the entrance to the sepulchre and put on it seven seals, pitched a tent and kept watch" (*Gos. Pet.* 8:31–33). The Greek of Matt 27:65 can be translated as "you have a guard," that is, the guard is Jewish, or "take a guard," that is, the guard is Roman, and the ambiguity may be a deliberate attempt by Matthew to leave it vague. He does not want any Jewish elders at the tomb but is willing, out of deference to the Passion-Resurrection Source, to leave it ambiguous whether the guards were Jewish or Roman.

Reaction at Tomb. In Matt 28:4 the reaction of the guards to the arrival of the angel and the opening of the tomb is rather negative: "And for fear of him the guards trembled and became like dead men." But their reaction in *Gos. Pet.* 10:38 is this: "When now those soldiers saw this, they awakened the centurion and the elders—for they were also there to assist at the watch." Their reaction is not at all as in Matt 28:4 but rather serves to ensure both Roman and Jewish authorities as official witnesses of the resurrection. The guards awaken both the centurion and the elders of the Jews in 10:38 so that they can see the actual resurrection in 10:39–42. Nobody sees the resurrection in Matthew, and certainly not the Jewish authorities.

Report from Tomb. In Matt 28:11–15 the guards report back to the Jewish authorities and are bribed into silence. Notice the slight discrepancy in that they report to the Jewish authortities but must be protected by them against Pilate in Matt 28:14. Matthew is being very careful to avoid precisely what *Peter* is saying, namely, that both Jewish and Roman authorities witnessed the resurrection of Jesus.

For *Peter*, of course, a Roman guard reports back to Pilate. But that is not the most interesting point of his narrative. Here is *Gos. Pet.* 11:45–49:

When *those who were of the centurion's company* saw this, they hastened by night to Pilate, abandoning the sepulchre which they were guarding, and reported everything that they had seen, being full of disquietude and saying, "In truth he was the Son of God," Pilate answered and said, "I am clean from the blood of the Son of God, upon such a thing have you decided." Then all came to him, beseeching him and urgently calling upon him to command the centurion and the soldiers to tell no one what they had seen. "For it is better for us," they said, "to make ourselves guilty of the greatest sin before God than to fall into the hands of the people of the Jews and be stoned." Pilate therefore commanded the centurion and the soldiers to say nothing.

There were two sets of authorities, Roman and Jewish, guarding the tomb in *Gos. Pet.* 8:31–33, witnessing the resurrection in 10:38–42, and reporting back to Pilate in 11:45–49. I shall look at them separately.

1) Jewish Authorities. I emphasize that it is the Jewish elders from the tomb who are involved in the phrases italicized above. Their designation there is similar to that in *Gos. Pet.* 8:32, "And all who were there, together with the centurion and the soldiers, rolled thither a great stone." For *Peter*, then, the Jewish authorities who have witnessed the resurrection are forced to confess in *Gos. Pet.* 11:45, "'In truth he was the Son of God.'" The narrative must next explain why they did not proclaim the event publicly. This continues and consummates the theme of Jewish People versus Jewish Authorities which runs throughout the Passion-Resurrection Source in *Peter*. In *GP 1: Resurrection and Deposition* the people experience the miraculous darkness at the death of Jesus, in 5:18. In *GP 3: Tomb and Burial* they repent and confess the righteousness of Jesus, in 7:25 and 8:28. In *GP 4: Resurrection and Confession*, then, the authorities must suppress the fact that they have crucified the Son of God, lest they be stoned by the people, in 11:48. They choose to commit this "greatest sin before God" rather than risk death.

2) Roman Authorities. But Pilate also confesses that Jesus

was the Son of God and insists that he, unlike the Jewish authorities to whom he is speaking, is innocent of Jesus' death. Pilate's innocence, symbolized by his Hand Washing, presumably in the missing verse preceding *Gos. Pet.* 1:1, and explicitly asserted here in 11:46, appears as a single unit in Matt 27:24. But whereas *Peter* has the Jewish authorities accepting guilt before God rather than death from the people, Matt 27:25 follows with the infamous, "And all the *people* answered, 'His blood be upon us and upon our children!'"

Both the Jewish and the Roman authorities confess that Jesus is the Son of God. But Pilate, at the request of the Jewish authorities, commands the soldiers to be silent so that the Jewish people will not know what happened and stone their leaders for what they had done. This both asserts that the resurrection engendered belief and explains why that belief was not proclaimed. I consider that Matt 28:4, 11–15 is a totally anti-Jewish redaction of this story in Peter *but* has no independent tradition whatsoever.

It has often been asserted that the *Gospel of Peter* is extremely pro-Roman and anti-Jewish and that this proves the late and dependent nature of its passion tradition. First, its trial involved, apparently, Pilate, Herod Antipas, and the Jewish authorities. Second, Pilate is certainly much less guilty than in the intracanonical gospels since Herod is clearly in charge of the crucifixion. This avoids their conflict between a Pilate who admits Jesus' innocence but still condemns him to death. At this stage, by the way, I consider it an open question who was in charge of the crucifixion, Pilate and the Roman authorities or Herod and the Jewish authorities. Third, there is a clear distinction made between Jewish people and Jewish authorities in the Passion-Resurrection Source, and the latter are repeatedly afraid of the former. Vestiges of this last point are still evident in Luke 23:48. But, apart from that, the intracanonical gospels, while asserting Pilate's reluctance, still keep him in charge and they indict with equal vehemence both Jewish prople and Jewish authorities. The Passion-Resurrection Source had a different vision.

DISCIPLES AND APPARITION

I termed *GP 4* both *Resurrection and Confession* because the Passion-Resurrection Source originally ended with the confession of both Jewish and Roman authorities that Jesus was the Son of God. This is not, of course, the way the story ends in Matthew, Luke, or John. There the final vision of the Risen Lord is to the apostles and it gives them their mandate to mission.

I consider that *GP 6: Disciples and (?) Apparition* was taken by the final redactor from John 21:1–8, that it was prepared for by the preliminary insert of *Gos. Pet.* 7:26–27, and that its primary purpose was to establish the pseudepigraphical authorship and authority of Simon Peter for the new *Gospel of Peter*. Since the text breaks off at 14:60 there is little direct evidence that can be offered for the dependence of *Gos. Pet.* 14:58–60 on John 21:1–8. I am persuaded, however, by the fact that this seems to fit into the pattern already established for the insertions of *GP 2* and *5* into the originally closed unity of the Passion-Resurrection Source of *GP 1–3–4*.

This pattern is the preliminary insert in *Gos. Pet.* 7:26–27. First, this breaks into the sequence of 7:25 + 8:28 which details how the repentance in 7:25 led to the request for guards in 8:28. Second, it states, "But I mourned with my fellows, and being wounded in heart we hid ourselves, for we were sought after by them as *evildoers* and as persons who wanted to set fire to the temple. Because of all these things we were fasting and sat mourning and weeping night and day until the Sabbath." Notice, by the way, the italicized expression "evildoers" (*kakourgoi*), borrowed, I presume, from the original "malefactors" (*kakourgoi*) of *Gos. Pet.* 4:10, 13. The main point, however, is that "night and day until the Sabbath" is a very strange expression to use at the very eve of the Sabbath: recall 2:5 and 9:34. What has happened is that the final redactor in writing this phrase is already looking forward to the Sabbath after, not before, Easter, to the Sabbath of 14:58–59, "Now it was the last day of unleavened bread and many went away and repaired to their homes, since the feast was at an end. But we, the twelve disciples of the Lord, wept and mourned, and each one, very grieved for what had come to pass, went to his own home." He is thinking of a week of mourning which would be terminated only by the apparition of the Risen Lord to the disciples themselves.

Gos. Pet. 7:26–27 is the final preliminary insert of the three mentioned earlier. It jars its present context because it was intended to look forward and prepare for *GP 6*. That final unit presumably contained an apparition of the Risen Lord borrowed from John 21:1–8 but certainly served to bring the entire text under the aegis of Simon Peter. Where John 21:3 has "Simon Peter said to them, 'I am going fishing,'" *Gos. Pet.* 14:60 has, "But I, Simon Peter . . . "

RESURRECTION IN TRADITION

Transmission

There is one very obvious question which has not been asked nearly enough. The four intracanonical gosepls agree quite harmoniously in the sequence and detail of the passion narrative. But they disagree almost totally on the place and time, the setting and content of Jesus' apparition to the apostles to give them their missionary mandate for the world. If both those traditions are based on historical recall, why are they so radically different in result? Even if one concedes a certain disagreement due to the vagaries of human memory, why is that memory so very much better on the passion than on the resurrection? Surely, the details of that last meeting between the apostles and their Lord, that meeting wherein they received

179

their mandate to worldwide mission, was at least as memorable as the details of the passion.

My own answer to that question should be clear by now. The agreement on the passion narrative in the four intracanonical gospels stems from the fact that they all have a common origin in the Passion-Resurrection Source. Mark himself used this text, and the other three intracanonical gospels used only it and Mark for their own compositions. No wonder, then, that they have remarkably similar accounts of the passion.

Exactly the opposite happened with regard to the resurrection narrative. Once again, the earliest tradition is that of the Passion-Resurrection Source. But Mark was totally unwilling to accept this account. He relocated it into his Transfiguration scene at 9:2–8 and replaced it with the Women and Tomb scene at 16:1–8. That left the other three intracanonical gospels on their own. They could not end their gospels, as Mark had done, with the harsh negativity of the empty tomb, but neither could they follow the model of the Passion-Resurrection Source and conclude with the climactic confession of the Son of God from both Jewish and Roman authorities. So they adopted and adapted Mark 16:1–8 into their own texts as Matt 28:1–8; Luke 23:1–11; and John 20:1, 11–13, but after that, they each went their own individual way.

It is the acceptance or rejection of the Passion-Resurrection Source that accounts for the unity of the passion and the diversity of the apparition narratives in the four intracanonical gospels.

Intertextuality

The Old Testament resonances and allusions so well documented by Jürgen Denker (58–77) for the passion narrative are not at all evident for the resurrection narrative in the Passion-Resurrection Source. There is, of course, the mention of "for three days" in *Gos. Pet.* 8:30. This recalls the "he was raised on the third day in accordance with the scriptures" of the early

RESURRECTION AND CONFESSION

creed in 1 Cor 15:4. Behind this, at least ultimately, is Hos 6:2, "After two days he will revive us; on the third day he will raise us up, that we may live before him." But, apart from that basic allusion, the resurrection description is not a product of intertextuality at all.

EPILOGUE

Just recently Helmut Koester said, "I want to challenge the scholarly world to write the literary history of the gospels in early Christianity considering all gospel materials which are available" (1983:62). This book is a partial and preliminary answer to that challenge and it has three main conclusions.

FOUR OTHER GOSPELS

The four extracanonical gospels in this book relate in almost all the ways possible to the intracanonical four. The *Gospel of Thomas* is a completely separate and parallel stream of the Jesus tradition. It is not dependent on the inner four and they are in no way dependent on it. They are parallel traditions. Moreover, there is something of a chasm set between them and it. The essential difference is not that it is heterodox and they orthodox but that it is a discourse gospel and they are narrative gospels. It is concerned only with the words of Jesus but they with the words and deeds, teachings and healings, life and death of Jesus. Egerton Papyrus 2 evinces a direct relationship with both John and Mark and the case studied in this book argues that Mark is dependent on it directly. What is fascinating about its fragments, besides the very early age, is that such a random sample shows a stage before the distinction of Johannine and Synoptic traditions was operative. The *Secret Gospel of Mark* is a somewhat similar but much more complicated case. Once again John, indirectly, and Mark, directly, know this narrative. It and our canonical Mark must come from the same school or even author, but canonical Mark has dismembered its units and redistributed them beyond recovery across his own text. Only with *Secret Mark* in front of you can you recognize that those many strange phrases in canonical Mark are the textual debris of units concerning the resurrection, baptism, and family of the

183

resurrected youth, from *Secret Mark*. Egerton Papyrus 2 and *Secret Mark* were both, however, in the tradition of narrative rather than discourse gospels. They are concerned not only with the words but also with the deeds of Jesus. The relations between the fourth example, the *Gospel of Peter*, and the intra-canonical four are as complicated as that of the *Gospel of Thomas* is simple. Its present content is both independent of them and dependent on them. The core is the Passion-Resurrection Source which is earlier than and independent of the intracanonical gospels. Indeed, all four of them know and use this source. But the final *Gospel of Peter* attempts to preserve that independent tradition by uniting with it units from the intracanonical gospels and placing the new complex under the pseudepigraphical authority of Peter. This is similar to what happened with the gospel of John, except, of course, that it succeeded in gaining canonicity and *Peter* did not.

One conclusion, then, is that scholarly discussion on those four texts needs some rather radical revision.

WORD AND EVENT

My own essential interest, however, is not just with which text bred which other text, and least of all with finding some pristine text still wet with the dews of dawn. What fascinates me is the hermeneutical process at work in all this. The cases I studied involved both parable and miracle, passion and resurrection. And exactly the same interpretational process was at work in all those cases.

Take, for example, the process of intertextuality. On the one hand, there is intertextuality from earlier Old Testament texts. The interpretation of Jesus' parable concerning The *Evil Tenants* involved an infiltration from earlier texts such as Ps 188:22–23 and Isa 5:1–7 into the very narrative fabric of the story. This intertextuality created a new story as an interpretation of the original story. But that was exactly the same process seen in the passion and burial traditions. The narrative about Jesus' passion and crucifixion, as also about his burial and guarding by the authorities was built up not from details of historical recall but from the intertextuality of biblical prophecy. Texts from Isaiah and the Psalms, Deuteronomy and Joshua, for instance, created the narrative fabric of the passion and burial, just as those from Isaiah and the Psalms created the narrative fabric of *The Evil Tenants* parable. On the other hand, there is intertextuality from later Christian experiences. The interpretation of Jesus' parable concerning *The Great Supper* involved an infiltration from later communal experiences of church life into the very narrative fabric of the story. Once again, the intertextuality of life in the Lukan or Matthean communities created new stories as interpretations of the original story. But that is the same process which happened within the resurrection traditions. The Passion-Resurrection Source describes a moment when the Jewish people and Roman authorities could be seen quite positively and even the Jewish authorities know the truth but hide it for fear of their own people. Miraculous resurrection begets immediate faith and there is no mention of apostles or preaching, mission or mandate. Thereafter, just as the communal vision of *Thomas*, Luke, or Matthew, dictated the interpretational content of *The Great Supper*, so did the varied communal experiences of Markan, Matthean, Lukan, or Johannine communities dictate the interpretational content of their resurrection and apparition traditions.

In the Jesus tradition, therefore, both word and event develop along the same twin trajectories of intertextuality from earlier Jewish texts and later Christian experiences.

Take, as another example, the expansion, contraction, relocation, and elimination of elements and units within parable and miracle, passion and resurrection. Interpretational expansion and contraction are very evident, respectively, in the parable of *The Great Supper*, say from Luke to Matthew, or that of *The Evil Tenants*, say from Matthew to Luke, but they are equally evident as the crucifixion details are increased or the resurrectional confession is decreased, say from the Passion-Resurrection Source to Mark. Interpretational relocation and elimination were the way canonical Mark solved the problems of *Secret Mark* but it was also the way he solved the resurrectional apparition in the Passion-Resurrection Source. He relocated it to the Transfiguration and replaced it with the Women at the Tomb. It was also the way the intracanonical gospels moved from Jesus' burial by enemies to inadequate burial by Joseph and on to magnificent burial by Nicodemus.

In the Jesus tradition, therefore, such processes as expansion and contraction, relocation and elimination, work in exactly similar ways on parable and miracle, on passion and resurrection.

PARABLE AND GOSPEL

Is it possible now to go one step further? As far as we can tell from contemporary sources which are dated with some accuracy, parables as a primary teaching method were quite particular to Jesus. These are realistic narratives true to the possibilities and actualities of everyday life. *The Evil Tenants,* for example, could easily have happened and may even have happened among rebellious peasantry and absentee landlords in Galilee. But this core of realism cannot turn parable into history. It simply sharpens the challenge of parable and the necessity of interpretation. The parable deals with word and deed, with life and death, and its format is that of realistic and biographical fiction. It is not history but neither is it lecture. The narrative gospel, as distinct from the discourse gospel, seems the better heir of this parabolic parentage. The discourse gospel focuses on the words of Jesus alone. The narrative gospel focuses on words and deeds, on teachings and healings, on passion and resurrection. It deals with a person's totality and it does so in a format that looks like biography and history but is actually parable and fiction. Of course it is based on historical facts, both possibilities and actualities, but so also are the parables.

My final conclusions may be stated as questions. Is there an essential formal continuity between the full realism of the parables spoken by Jesus and the narrative gospels written about Jesus? Is the narrativity of Jesus' parables a formal and stylistic warrant for Catholic Christianity's choice of narrative gospels as against Gnostic Christianity's preference for discourse gospels? Is the basic continuity between historical Jesus and ecclesiastical Christ established not so much in discussions about orthodox and heterodox contents as in the fictional realism with which Jesus spoke in parables and with which they spoke about him as parable itself?

WORKS CONSULTED

ANF   See Roberts, Donaldson, & Coxe.

Attridge, Harold W.
1979   "The Original Text of Gos. Thom., Saying 30." *Bulletin of the American Society of Papyrologists* 16:153–57.

Barnard, L. W.
1968   "The Origins and Emergence of the Church in Edessa during the First Two Centuries A.D." *Vigiliae Christianae* 22:161–75.

Bauer, Walter
1971   *Orthodoxy and Heresy in Earliest Christianity.* 2nd ed. Philadelphia: Fortress Press.

Bell, H. Idriss
1949   "The Gospel Fragments P. Egerton 2." *HTR* 42:53–63. [Review of Mayedo's Marburg dissertation; see below]

Bell, H. Idriss, & T. C. Skeat
1935a   *Fragments of an Unknown Gospel and Other Early Christian Papyri.* London: Trustees of the British Museum (Oxford University Press). [Pp. 1–41: "Unknown Gospel"; see also Plates I & II]
1935b   *The New Gospel Fragments.* London: Trustees of the British Museum (Oxford University Press).

Bouriant, Urbain
1892   "Fragments du texte grec du livre d'Enoch et de quelques écrits attribués a Saint Pierre." Pp. 137–42 in *Mémoires publiés par les membres de la Mission archéologique française au Caire* 9/1. Paris: Libraire de la Société asiatique.

Brown, Raymond E.
1974   "The Relation of 'The Secret Gospel of Mark' to the Fourth Gospel." *CBQ* 36:466–85.

Browne, G. M., *et alii*
1972   *The Oxyrhynchus Papyri.* Volume XLI. London: Egypt Exploration Society. [R. A. Coles edited Oxy P 2949 = *Gos. Pet. 2,* on pp. 15–16; see also Plate II]

Butterworth, George William
1919   *Clement of Alexandria: The Exhortation to the Greeks; The Rich Man's Salvation; To the Newly Baptized.* LCL 92. Cambridge, MA: Harvard University Press.

FOUR OTHER GOSPELS

Cameron, Ron
1982   *The Other Gospels. Non-Canonical Gospel Texts.* Philadelphia: Westminster.
Carlston, Charles Edwin
1961   "Transfiguration and Resurrection." *JBL* 80:233–40.
Cěrný, Jaroslav
1952   *Paper and Books in Ancient Egypt.* Chicago: Ares.
Charles, R. H.
1900   *The Ascension of Isaiah.* London: Black.
Collins, Adela Yarbro
1979   "The Early Christian Apocalypses." Pp. 61–121 in *Semeia* 14 (1979): *Apocalypse. The Morphpology of a Genre.* Ed. John J. Collins.
Crossan, John Dominic
1976   "Empty Tomb and Absent Lord (Mark 16:1–8)." Pp. 135–52 in *The Passion in Mark. Studies on Mark 14–16.* Ed. Werner H. Kelber. Philadelphia: Fortress Press.
Davies, Stevan L.
1983   *The Gospel of Thomas and Christian Wisdom.* New York: Seabury Press.
Denker, Jürgen
1975   *Die theologiegeschichtliche Stellung des Petrusevangeliums. Ein Beitrag zur Frühgeschichte des Doketismus.* Europäische Hochschulschriften 23:36. Bern/Frankfurt: Lang.
de Solages, B.
1979   "L'Evangile de Thomas et les Evangiles Canoniques: L'Ordre des Péricopes." *Bulletin de littérature ecclésiastique* 80:102–8.
Dodd, Charles Harold
1953   "A New Gospel." Pp. 12–52 in Dodd, *New Testament Studies.* Manchester: Manchester University Press. =*Bulletin of the John Rylands Library* 20 (1936) 56–92.
Fitzmyer, J. A.
1971   "The Oxyrhynchus Logoi of Jesus and the Coptic Gospel according to Thomas." Pp. 355–433 in Fitzmyer, *Essays on the Semitic Background of the New Testament.* London: Chapman.
Gardner-Smith, P.
1925–26a "The Gospel of Peter." *JTS* 27:255–71.
1925–26b "The Date of the Gospel of Peter." *JTS* 27:401–7.

Grenfell, Bernard P., & Arthur S. Hunt
  1897   ΛΟΓΙΑ ΙΗΣΟΥ: *Sayings of Our Lord from an Early Greek Papyrus*. London: Egypt Exploration Fund (New York: Frowde).
  1898   *The Oxyrhynchus Papyri. Part I*. London: Egypt Exploration Fund.
  1900   *The Amherst Papyri. Part I: The Ascension of Isaiah, and Other Theological Fragments*. London: Frowde (Oxford University Press).
  1904a   *The Oxyrhynchus Papyri. Part IV*. London: Egypt Exploration Fund.
  1904b   *New Sayings of Jesus and Fragment of a Lost Gospel from Oxyrhynchus*. London: Egypt Exploration Fund.

Hennecke, Edgar, & Wilhelm Schneemelcher
  1963–65 *New Testament Apocrypha* [=NTA]. 2 vols. Philadelphia: Westminster.

Howard, George
  1981   *The Teaching of Addai*. SBLTT 16. Chico, CA: Scholars Press.

Johnson, Benjamin A.
  1966   *Empty Tomb Tradition in the Gospel of Peter*. Th.D. dissertation, Harvard University.

Jonas, Hans
  1958   *The Gnostic Religion. The Message of the Alien God and the Beginnings of Christianity*. Boston, MA: Beacon Press.

Kelber, Werner H.
  1974   *The Kingdom in Mark*. Philadelphia: Fortress Press.
  1976   "Conclusion: From Passion Narrative to Gospel." Pp. 153–80 in *The Passion in Mark. Studies on Mark 14–16*. Ed. Werner H. Kelber. Philadelphia: Fortress Press.

Klijn, A. F. J.
  1962   "The 'Single One' in the Gospel of Thomas." *JBL* 81:271–78.

Koester, Helmut
  1980   "Apocryphal and Canonical Gospels." *HTR* 73:105–30.
  1983   "History and Development of Mark's Gospel (From Mark to *Secret Mark* and 'Canonical' Mark)." Pp. 35–57 in *Colloquy on New Testament Studies. A Time for Reappraisal and Fresh Approaches*. Ed. Bruce Corley. Macon, GA: Mercer University Press. [Pp. 59–85: "Seminar Dialogue with Helmut Koester"]

Lake, Kirsopp
1912–13   *The Apostolic Fathers*. 2 vols. LCL 24–25. Cambridge, MA: Harvard University Press.

Lake, Kirsopp, & John Ernest Oulton
1926–32   *Eusebius: The Ecclesiastical History*. 2 vols. LCL 153 & 265. Cambridge, MA: Harvard University Press.

Lindars, Barnabas
1961   *New Testament Apologetic. The Doctrinal Significance of the Old Testament Quotations*. Philadelphia: Westminster.

Lods, A.
1893   "Reproduction en héliogravure du manuscrit d'Enoch et des écrits attribués a Saint Pierre." Pp. 219–24, with Plates II–VI, in *Mémoires publiés par les membres de la Mission archéologique française au Caire* 9/3. Paris: Libraire de la Société asiatique.

Lührmann, Dieter
1981   "POx 2949: EvPt 3–5 in einer Handschrift des 2./3. Jahrhunderts." *ZNW* 72:216–26.

MacRae, George W.
1978   "Nag Hammadi and the New Testament." Pp. 144–57 in *Gnosis. Festschrift für Hans Jonas*. Ed. B. Aland *et alii*. Göttingen: Vandenhoeck & Ruprecht.

1980   "Why the Church Rejected Gnosticism?" Pp. 126–33 in *Jewish and Christian Self-Definition*. Vol. 1: *The Shaping of Christianity in the Second and Third Centuries*. Ed. E. P. Sanders. Philadelphia: Fortress Press.

Maurer, Christian
1963–65   "The Gospel of Peter." Pp. 179–87 in *New Testament Apocrypha*. Vol. 1. Eds. Edgar Hennecke & Wilhelm Schneemelcher. Philadelphia: Westminster.

Mayeda, Goro
1946   *Das Leben-Jesu-Fragment Papyrus Egerton 2 und seine Stellung in der urchristlichen Literaturgeschichte*. Bern: Haupt.

McCant, Jerry W.
1984   "The Gospel of Peter: Docetism Reconsidered." *NTS* 30: 258–73.

Meeks, Wayne A.
1974   "The Image of the Androgyne: Some Uses of a Symbol in Earliest Christianity." *HR* 13:165–208.

Metzger, Bruce M.
  1971   *A Textual Commentary on the Greek New Testament.* New
              York: United Bible Societies.
  1977   *The Early Versions of the New Testament.* Oxford: Claren-
              don Press.
Neirynck, Frans
  1982a   "Duplicate Expressions in the Gospel of Mark." Pp. 83–142
              in *Evangelica. Collected Essays by Frans Neirynck.* Ed. F. Van
              Segbroeck. BETL 55. Leuven: Leuven University Press.
  1982b   "Les Femmes au Tombeau. Etude de la Rédaction Mat-
              théenne (Matt. XXVIII.1–10)." Pp. 273-296 in *Evangelica*
              (see 1982a).
NTA   See Hennecke & Schneemelcher.
Olrik, Axel
  1965   "Epic Laws of Folk Narrative." Pp. 129–41 in *The Study of
              Folklore.* Ed. Alan Dundes. Englewood Cliffs, NJ: Prentice-
              Hall. ="Epische Gesetze der Volksdichtung." *Zeitschrift für
              Deutsches Altertum* 51 (1909) 1–12.
Oulton, J. E. L., & Henry Chadwick
  1954   *Alexandrian Christianity.* The Library of Christian Classics
              2. Philadelphia: Westminster.
Quasten, J.
  1950–60   *Patrology.* 3 vols. Utrecht-Antwerp: Spectrum.
Quesnell, Quentin
  1975   "The Mar Saba Clementine: A Question of Evidence." *CBQ*
              37:48–67.
  1976   "A Reply to Morton Smith." *CBQ* 38:200–3.
Roberts, Alexander, James Donaldson, & A. Cleveland Coxe
  1926   *The Ante-Nicene Fathers.* American Reprint of the Edin-
              burgh Edition. 10 vols. New York: Scribner's.
Robinson, James M.
  1979a   "Introduction: What is the Nag Hammadi Library?" *Biblical
              Archeologist* 42:201–5.
  1979b   "The Discovery of the Nag Hammadi Codices." *Biblical
              Archeologist* 42:207–24
  1982   "Jesus: From Easter to Valentinus (or to the Apostles'
              Creed)." *JBL* 101:5–37.
Robinson, James M., & Helmut Koester
  1971   *Trajectories through Early Christianity.* Philadelphia: For-
              tress Press.

Rudolph, Kurt
1983   *Gnosis. The Nature and History of Gnosticism.* Trans. P. W. Coxon & K. H. Kuhn. Trans. Ed. R. McL. Wilson. San Francisco, CA: Harper & Row.
Sieber, John H.
1966   *A Redactional Analysis of the Synoptic Gospels with Regard to the Question of the Sources of the Gospel according to Thomas.* Ann Arbor, MI: University Microfilms International.
Smith, Dwight Moody
1979–80   "John and the Synoptics: Some Dimensions of the Problem." *NTS* 26:425–44.
Smith, Jonathan Z.
1965–66   "The Garments of Shame." *HR* 5:217–38.
Smith, Morton
1960   "Monasteries and their Manuscripts." *Archaeology* 13:172–77.
1973a   *The Secret Gospel. The Discovery and Interpretation of the Secret Gospel according to Mark.* New York: Harper & Row.
1973b   *Clement of Alexandria and a Secret Gospel of Mark.* Cambridge, MA: Harvard University Press.
1976   "On the Authenticity of the Mar Saba Letter of Clement." *CBQ* 38:196–99.
1982   "Clement of Alexandria and Secret Mark: The Score at the End of the First Decade." *HTR* 75:449–61.
Swete, Henry Barclay
1893   ΕΥΑΓΓΕΛΙΟΝ ΚΑΤΑ ΠΕΤΡΟΝ: *The Akhmîm Fragment of the Apocryphal Gospel of St. Peter.* London: Macmillan.
Talley, Thomas J.
1982   "Liturgical Time in the Ancient Church: The State of Research." *Studia Liturgica* 14:34–51.
Turner, John D.
1975   *The Book of Thomas the Contender.* SBLDS 2. Missoula, MT: Scholars Press.
Walter, Nikolaus
1972–73   "Eine vormatthäische Schilderung der Auferstehung Jesu." *NTS* 19:415–29.
Wilson, Robert McL.
1982   "Nag Hammadi and the New Testament." *NTS* 28:289–302.

Wisse, Frederik
  1971   "The Nag Hammadi Library and the Heresiologists."
          Vigiliae Christianae 25:205–23.
  1978   "Gnosticism and Early Monasticism in Egypt." Pp. 431–40
          in *Gnosis. Festschrift für Hans Jonas.* Ed. B. Aland *et alii.*
          Göttingen: Vandenhoeck & Ruprecht.

INDEX OF AUTHORS

INDEX

INDEX OF CITATIONS

8:38 115	20:22 72, 81
8:54 113	20:24 82
9:28 116	20:24-26 82
9:30 113, 167	20:25 83
9:42 113	22:53 116
9:51 118	23:1-11 180
10:30-35 41	23:6-12 137, 142
11:33 36	23:6-48 145, 146
12:3 36	23:9 147
12:46 49	23:25b 137
13:28-29 49	23:32 143
14:1-2 46	23:33 143
14:1-6 43	23:33b 137
14:1-14 43	23:34b 137
14:7-11 43	23:35 143
14:12-14 43, 46	23:36 137, 139
14:13 45	23:38 137
14:15 46	23:39 143
14:15-24 43, 56	23:39-43 137, 142, 143
14:16-17 43	23:44 150
14:16-24 39, 43, 46	23:44a 137
14:18-20 44	23:44b 137
14:21 45	23:46 137
14:21-24 45	23:47 140, 141
16:1-7 60	23:48 151, 177
16:8b 60	23:50-51 155
17:14 71	23:50-52 152
18:18-23 115	23:53 152, 157
18:21 115	23:54-56 157
18:23 115	24:1 155, 157, 158, 160
18:29 45	24:1-11 162
18:38 112	24:2 112, 158
19:26-27 49	24:3-5a 158
19:28-29 112	24:4 113, 167
20:9 58	24:5b-8 158
20:9-18 53, 56, 58	24:6-8 160
20:13-15a 58	24:9-11 158
20:15b-16 58	24:12 162, 163
20:16 58	John
20:18 59	2:4 71
20:20-26 77, 80	3:1 157

INDEX